ANTI-SAINTS

ANTI-

Translation and Introduction by Sheila Delany

SAINTS

The *New Golden Legend* of Sylvain Maréchal

 THE UNIVERSITY OF ALBERTA PRESS

Published by
The University of Alberta Press
Ring House 2
Edmonton, Alberta, Canada T6G 2E1
www.uap.ualberta.ca

Copyright © 2012 Sheila Delany

Library and Archives Canada Cataloguing in Publication

Maréchal, Sylvain, 1750-1803
[Nouvelle légende dorée]
    Anti-saints : the new golden legend of Sylvain
Maréchal / translation and introduction by Sheila Delany.

Translation of: Nouvelle légende dorée, ou, Dictionnaire des saintes.
Includes bibliographical references.
ISBN 978-0-88864-604-0

    1. Christian women saints—Biography—Dictionaries—Early works to 1800.
2. Christian women saints—Anecdotes—Early works to 1800. 3. Christian women
saints—Humor—Early works to 1800. 4. Religious satire, French—Early works
to 1800. I. Delany, Sheila II. Title. III. Nouvelle légende dorée.

BX4656.M3713 2011   270.2092'2   C2011-906306-9

First edition, first printing, 2012.
Printed and bound in Canada by Houghton Boston Printers, Saskatoon, Saskatchewan.
Copyediting and Proofreading by Lesley Peterson.

All rights reserved. No part of this publication may be produced, stored in a retrieval
system, or transmitted in any form or by any means (electronic, mechanical,
photocopying, recording, or otherwise) without prior written consent. Contact the
University of Alberta Press for further details.

The University of Alberta Press is committed to protecting our natural environment.
As part of our efforts, this book is printed on Enviro Paper: it contains 100% post-
consumer recycled fibres and is acid- and chlorine-free.

The University of Alberta Press gratefully acknowledges the support received for its
publishing program from The Canada Council for the Arts. The University of Alberta
Press also gratefully acknowledges the financial support of the Government of Canada
through the Canada Book Fund (CBF) and the Government of Alberta through the
Alberta Multimedia Development Fund (AMDF) for its publishing activities.

This book has been published with the help of a grant from the Canadian Federation
for the Humanities and Social Sciences, through the Aid to Scholarly Publications
Program, using funds provided by the Social Sciences and Humanities Research
Council of Canada.

CONTENTS

ACKNOWLEDGMENTS
vii

INTRODUCTION
1

TRANSLATOR'S NOTE
25

ANTI-SAINTS A – Z
27

DEDICATORY EPISTLE...
29

APPENDIX
145

CHRONOLOGY
147

NOTES
153

BIBLIOGRAPHY
169

ACKNOWLEDGMENTS

I'd like to acknowledge the help of librarians at Stanford's Special Collections and Berkeley's Bancroft Special Collections libraries, Yale's Beinecke Rare Books and Manuscripts Library, the New York Public Library, the Vancouver Art Gallery library, the Sutro Library in San Francisco, and especially Vera Yuen and Ivana Niseteo at the Simon Fraser University library. Professor Earl Jeffrey Richards of Muenster University offered valuable bibliographical advice. Thanks, too, to my SFU research assistants along the way: Derrick Higginbotham, Jean Stadnicki Leggett, Stefania Forlini, and Wes Reamsbottom. The generosity of Canada's Social Sciences and Humanities Research Council enabled me to consult much of Maréchal's work in original editions as well as radical journals of his day and other documents at the libraries above; that of the Camargo Foundation provided ideal conditions in Cassis, France, in which to write the Introduction. The contribution of the University Publications Fund at Simon Fraser University toward the production of this book is also appreciated.

To Charles Muscatine, Laurie Finke, and David Gay, special appreciation and gratitude for their scholarly and personal example, encouragement, and support in this and other projects. Judith, Jane, Kitty, Lynn, David, Malcolm, Jean and Blair, Wayne: your conversation, counsel, and tech expertise at home and away meant a lot and helped keep the balance—which, as every scholar and writer knows, isn't always easy. Last but far from least, the sharp-eyed and sharp-witted Lesley Peterson, copyeditor for the University of Alberta Press, tweaked this into a better book. Merci à tous et toutes!

P.S. Between the writing and the publication of these acknowledgments, Professor Muscatine passed away in March 2010, at the age of eighty-nine. He had recently published a new book, on education, and never lost his sense of elegance, fun or hospitality. He is missed by many; his influence survives in the work of former students and his personal example in those who knew him.

INTRODUCTION

On Monday, September 14, 1789, the radical journal *Révolutions de Paris* (*RdeP*) covered a local event of some public interest:

> Occupé des intérêts puissans de la nation, nous avions renoncé à parler de ces fêtes militaires, de ces processions, objets d'amusemens & de luxe, que chaque jour on voit renouveller dans cette capitale; car si le pain & les loix nous manquent, du moins le faste & la dévotion nous consolent. Aujourd'hui, cependant, il se présente une de ces processions qui attire l'attention publique: ce sont les citoyens gardes nationaux des districts du fauxbourg Saint-Antoine qui se sont réunis, ayant à leur tête les jeunes vierges de ces cantons, dont le cortége nombreux va faire bénir à Sainte-Genevieve, & mettre sous la protection de cette patrone de la capitale, un modele de la bastille. Ce modele, de la hauteur de quatre pieds ou environ... rappelle le moment du siege de cette forteresse...Ici l'on a tout imité, les armes, les hommes, le [sic] drapeaux, les canons, & ce modele a produit toute l'illusion que l'on pouvait en attendre.

> Occupied with powerful national matters, we have omitted to speak about those military celebrations and processions, objects of amusement and expense, which are every day seen to proliferate in this capital; for if bread and laws are lacking, at least splendor and devotion console us. Today, though, one of those parades is presented that draws public attention: it is the national-guard citizens from neighborhoods in the Saint-Antoine suburb who have reunited, headed by young virgins of those neighborhoods; their numerous cortège is going to bless Saint Genevieve and place under the protection of this patron

saint of the capital a model of the Bastille. This model, about four feet high...recalls the moment of the siege of this fortress... Here they imitated everything, the weapons, the men, the flags, the cannons, and this model produced every effect one might expect from it.

Although anonymous, the article was probably written by Sylvain Maréchal, an editor of the journal from late 1790 through its demise in 1794.[1] Maréchal's distinctive style is not hard to spot; it appears he had what we might call "the women, culture and religion desk" at the journal. Typical in style and sentiment of Maréchal is the sardonic critique of the current revolutionary government for its attempt to pacify a hungry and impatient working population with elaborate spectacle; indeed that is a recurrent theme in his work. Also typical is the development of the article into an encomium on liberty with its references to Greece, Rome and "l'immortel *Jean-Jacques*" (Rousseau), its exhortation to citizens to unite fearlessly once again, its denunciation of priests who visited innocent prisoners but did nothing to free them or even to improve their frightful conditions, becoming instead "les agens du plus horrible despotisme" ("agents of the most horrible despotism")—and, another Maréchal trait—its footnotes.

I choose this anecdote to begin because of its all too evident contradictions. On one hand, a mock-up of the medieval fortress-prison hated, assaulted and taken on July 14, 1789 by the armed population of Paris in what remains the best-known of many revolutionary *journées*, still celebrated annually in France as a national holiday and betokening the explosive beginnings of modern political life and the modern state. On the other, two oppressive early-medieval institutions—Catholic Church and monarchy—combined in the figure of Saint Genevieve, patron saint of Paris, whose prayers were said to have converted the fifth-century Frankish ruler, Clovis, to orthodox Christianity, thus producing the first Christian French monarch.

Such contradictions existed in uneasy equilibrium for years during and after the revolutionary period, and many would argue they still do. They characterize the revolution as a whole, or rather in its several phases, and they characterize Sylvain Maréchal, product of and participant in the political culture of his day.² The text I offer in this volume, in my translation, doesn't by itself illustrate that ambiguity, for its target is Catholicism, and Maréchal was perfectly clear about Catholicism. A militant atheist, he considered all organized religion to be anti-social, exploitative, unnatural, and psychologically damaging. It was therefore an appropriate object of ridicule and rejection, as the legendary amply shows. The following selective overview will, I hope, show the social ambiguities he channeled in his writing, and the *New Golden Legend*'s place in his life and work.

†

The text that most transparently expresses the personal and political contradictions both of the period and the author is a late one, published in 1801, two years before Maréchal's death. It is the *Projet d'une loi portant defense d'apprendre à lire aux femmes (Project for a Law Forbidding Women to Learn to Read)*, with its 113 reasons supporting that position. Recent interest in this work developed as part of the influence of French feminism and gender studies, particularly surrounding the 1989 celebrations of the two-hundredth anniversary of the beginning of the revolution. Yet despite this obnoxious treatise, Maréchal was married, apparently happily, to a devout Catholic whom he wed when he was forty-two and she twenty-eight. He had women friends, some of them writers and one of them an editor of his work (Fusil, 221). Two of them responded to the *Projet*, one taking it as a bad joke, the other not; and one of these friends, a feminist, was in the small group at his deathbed (Fraisse, 269). Incongruous as it seems, and is, for someone who considered himself an egalitarian to wish to consign women to illiteracy, even in jest, this was a more mainstream attitude than we may realize. Espousing essentialist concepts of "feminine nature," no revolutionary government enfranchised women or allowed them to serve in any public function despite various proposals from women and men, including political leaders, to do so (Condorcet, de Gouges): women were simply not made for the rough political life. The legendary doesn't directly address issues of education and literacy. If it wants to free women from religion it is so that they may become good wives, mothers and citizens; educate their children in moral values; perform charitable works; if necessary, bear arms in defense of their country. This, despite the active participation of women, including organizing and fighting, in key political events, the rural and urban labor they performed, the presence of women's journals and political clubs,[3] women artists and writers in all genres, and ongoing public debate on the role and education of women in a new "querelle des femmes." In this context one can accurately characterize the *Projet* as reactionary, i.e., looking backward, not forward.[4] Nor was this ambivalence about women limited to the revolutionary era, for Frenchwomen waited until 1944 to achieve the vote. Even for men, suffrage remained a much-debated issue, with property and financial qualifications not resolved until well into the next century.

On the other hand, the revolutionary regime did establish free divorce more or less on demand (a law overturned by Napoleon in 1816), eliminated some of the despotic power of husbands over the person and property of wives, and decreed a range of laws protecting soldiers' wives, single mothers and their children. Maréchal favored these laws—he believed they would strengthen the marital bond—yet at the same time he deplored the action of a women's delegation petitioning the National Assembly for passage of those same laws (*RdeP* #143:20-24 for March 31-April 7, 1792).

The ambiguities observable at many levels of discourse and legislation stem, I suggest, from the multi-faceted nature and needs of the class coming into political power: the bourgeoisie big and small, mercantile and financial, quasi-aristocratic and administrative, landowning and industrial, judicial, academic and commercial. Complicating matters even further is an ambivalent relationship between the new middle-class government and the equally multi-faceted working populations of cities, especially Paris, and other regions of the country. These — the peasants, porters, servants, artisans, small shopkeepers both urban and rural — demanded, initiated, or carried out many components of the revolutionary movement, in its earlier period especially. But their deep needs, surpassing or contradicting those of the middle classes, could not at the time be met; the expression of those needs was soon both legally and militarily suppressed.

INTRODUCTION

†

Despite its significance, the *Projet* doesn't by itself define Maréchal, for he was a prolific author in many genres and with many strings to his bow. Born in 1750 into the Catholic family of a Parisian wine-merchant, he trained and briefly worked in law, but as a stutterer chose instead to devote himself to books as student, writer, and caretaker. Early on, he became a lifelong militant atheist and a poet, often imitating classical genres in pastoral-erotic or moral verse. Appointed assistant librarian at the prestigious Mazarin Library in Paris, the young scholar-poet gained access to a vast collection of classical, historical and religious material. A 1784 parody of biblical psalms and prophets, *Le livre échappé au déluge* (*The Book That Survived the Flood*), which denounced the rich, the clergy, hypocrites, royalty, prideful academics, war, and the judicial system, cost him this job.

The book opens with a Rabelaisian "notice historique" about the author of these newly-discovered psalms. It was a difficult birth, as he didn't want to be born into such a corrupt time and place. At birth he said, "Que ferai-je sur la Terre? J'y arrive beaucoup trop tard" ("What will I do on earth? I'm arriving much too late"). Having spoken too young, he remained a stutterer the rest of his life, a man whose "idole" was "la douce médiocrité" ("sweet/gentle middle-of-the-road"). This 1784 work deepened the skeptical-atheistic sensibility already expressed in the 1781 *Fragmens d'un poeme moral sur dieu*, which inverts any expectations that might be created by its title.[5] The *Fragmens* proclaims virtue in place of God, offering the Feuerbachian-Marxian notion that "L'homme a dit: faisons Dieu, qu'il soit à notre image! Dieu fut; et l'ouvrier adora son ouvrage" ("Man said: Let us make God in our image. God was, and the worker adored his work." Epigraph). In 1784, the perspective on God remains materialist: "Oui, mon Dieu! Tu existes: car j'ai tant besoin que tu existes! J'ai besoin de l'avenir, pour me faire supporter le présent. J'ai besoin d'un père, pour me défendre contre mes frères" ("Yes, my God, you exist, for I so much need you to exist! I need the future so that I can tolerate the present. I need a father, to defend myself against my brothers"). His "Dieu nul ou complice des crimes" ("God worthless or accomplice to crimes") resembles Blake's "Old Nobodaddy."

Some four years later, another work cost Maréchal his liberty. This was the *Almanach des honnêtes gens* (*Almanac of Upright People*), a calendar using the format of an old and still very popular genre. But whereas the usual almanac would start with January, note the Catholic holidays, offer useful information whether astronomical, agricultural, medical, etc., and mark each day with its appropriate saint, this one made innovations. It began with March, in accordance with the author's commitment to nature as norm and his rejection of a calendrical scheme sponsored by Roman Empire and Catholic Church, and it made each month thirty days long. It gave rationalistic numerical names to the months (e.g., June is "Quartile," February becomes "Duodécembre") and proposed, for extra days to make up the full 365, "solemnités purement morales": virtuous holidays such as a "Fête de l'amour" in spring or a celebration of "Reconnoissance" ("Gratitude") in autumn or of "Amitié" ("Friendship") in winter.

Far worse, in the eyes of civil and ecclesiastical authorities, was that this almanac marked the birth and death days not of Catholic saints and martyrs but of famous people of both sexes from other cultures and religions, many with what a traditional Catholic culture must consider dubious or outright subversive reputations. It was far from being an anti-royalist or anti-aristocratic collection, for numerous nobles, royals and other rulers appear: Elizabeth I of England, Alfred the Great, several Roman emperors and Ottoman rulers. But first in line, on March 1, is Moses, followed by Saladin on the 4th; Jesus Christ is noted for April 3 and Mahomet for June 7, so that Christianity, Judaism and Islam are given equal status; this, the author explains, is an example of "un lien commun de fraternité" ("a shared link of fraternity"). The presence of Jan Hus, the late-medieval Czech reformer, burnt at the stake for heresy, would further offend religious sensibilities. England, France's great colonial rival throughout the century, to whom vast territories in North America and India had been lost, is well represented with philosophers and poets (Bacon, Shakespeare, Newton, Milton, Dryden, Swift, Pope, and others). Particularly provocative in a colonial context would have been the cartographer/naval commander James Cook, who helped expand England's Pacific territories and had been instrumental in the British victory over the French in Canada. The collection is determinedly internationalist, featuring great artists of other countries – Cervantes, Michelangelo, da Vinci, Tasso, Petrarch, Albert Dürer, Handel – alongside such giants of French culture as Descartes, Boileau, Corneille, Voltaire and Rousseau. The political thrust of this almanac is even more clearly revealed by some of its commemorations: the Edict of Nantes (1588), which granted limited rights to Protestants, a still-controversial issue in 1788; the death of Spartacus, slave leader of a slave rebellion against the Romans; Brutus's assassination of Caesar; the expulsion of King Tarquin from Rome. Last but not least to offend was the feminine component of the calendar. While a few royal women appear, so do Agnès Sorel, the mistress of Charles VII who set the fashion for bare bosoms at the fifteenth-century court; Héloïse, the eleventh-century nun who refused to repent her passion for her lover and husband, the philosopher-priest Abelard; and Ninon de l'Enclos, the seventeenth-century courtesan and literary lady.

Reaction was rapid and severe: the author was flung into prison, though released after three months through the influence of close friends and relatives. The book was condemned by Parlement to be publicly "laceré et brulé" ("torn to pieces and burnt") as a scandalous, monstrous, miserable, sacrilegious and blasphemous production, full of impiety, atheism and folly, tending to destroy religion and good morals (Parlementary document in *Almanach*). Yet despite a ban on sales of the book – or, one might guess, because of it – Maréchal's almanac became a bestseller. Its price rose dramatically, as he relates (*RdeP* #212:108) and probably made the author rich; it generated many imitations (some of them obscene and incorrectly attributed to Maréchal). The Paris Commune in October 1793 adopted Maréchal's calendar (Fusil, 62), but the Convention – the national governmental body – did not, so a new republican calendar was composed, certainly indebted to Maréchal's.

Two multi-volume scholarly collaborations with artist and engraver François-Anne David occupied some time: the *Antiquités d'Herculanum* (1780), describing artworks in the recently discovered archaeological site near Pompeii, and the self-explanatory *Le Muséum de Florence* (1791), for both of which David did the engravings and Maréchal the (often rather prudish) explanatory text. A religious parody, the *Catéchisme du curé Meslier* (1790), deconstructed prayer by ridiculing it in question-and-answer form to yield atheistic answers that Maréchal sardonically associated with the real-life atheist priest Meslier.

Toward the end of 1790, Maréchal took on a co-editorship at *Révolutions de Paris* and helped build it into one of the most influential of the radical journals. This is the year of publication of the *Légende*, and although the short-lived dechristianization campaign was still two years in the future, the text anticipated it, much as the *Almanach* had anticipated the new official calendar. There was significant anti-clerical, though not necessarily anti-religious, sentiment in Paris and elsewhere, due to obvious moral and financial abuses by clergy. Though Catholicism remained the dominant and, pragmatically though not legally, the official religion in France, nonetheless this same year saw the start of the appropriation and sale of ecclesiastical property; Latreille comments that the government lived ten years from this transfer of wealth, and fought the war as well, against the several powers that invaded or tried to invade the country (1:92). Also in 1790, new religious vows were made illegal, although monks were permitted to remain in their establishments until death, and hospitals or teaching institutions remained; small establishments were combined; nuns who left their convents were given pensions. In November, the Civil Constitution of the Clergy was decreed: a set of regulations meant to eliminate abuses by reorganizing clerical structures and procedures. This was followed by the loyalty oath required of all clergy, to support "loi et roi." It was thus a propitious year for the appearance of such a text as Maréchal's.

1793 might have seemed a similarly propitious year for a writer of Maréchal's pro-revolutionary, anti-royalist (indeed tyrannicidal) and atheistic convictions, for it opened with the execution of King Louis XVI on January 21 and continued with other events suiting a radical perspective. In June, the moderate Girondin party were expelled from the Convention (the governmental body) and subsequently executed, leaving the more radical Jacobins in control and their leader, Maximilien Robespierre, with considerable influence. A new constitution was approved;[6] the new revolutionary calendar was introduced; price controls were decreed as the Parisian working people had demanded. The Terror officially began in September, defined by Robespierre as "prompt, severe, inflexible justice" for internal enemies

INTRODUCTION

(Žižek in Robespierre, *Virtue and Terror*, viii). Hundreds of hoarders and speculators in foodstuffs or other essentials, people with noble or royalist connections or sympathies, and many others denounced for, or simply suspected of, anti-revolutionary behavior or sentiments, went to the guillotine or to prison. The dechristianization movement, though unofficial and unevenly manifested across the country, was implementing various anti-clerical or anti-religious events in many places during the winter. On November 7, the Jacobin bishop of Paris, J.-B. Gobel, abdicated his office in a spectacular renunciation before the Convention. On November 10, the festival of Liberty and Reason was celebrated in Nôtre Dame Cathedral in Paris; Maréchal helped organize it and spoke at it (Fusil, 145). Counter-revolutionary revolts amounting to civil war in the north-west and south-east were suppressed during the winter, and in December, the British were driven out of Toulon, on the Mediterranean, by an artillery commanded by the young Napoleon Bonaparte. Although at first the revolution had aimed at a constitutional monarchy, the intervening three years had produced intensifying polarization and indeed treasonous behavior on the part of the royal couple, particularly the queen, who hoped to crush the revolution and regain absolute power with the help of foreign invaders. She was executed on October 16, 1793.

Two days later, Maréchal's play, *Le jugement dernier des rois* (*The Last Judgment of Kings*), opened at the Théâtre de la République (formerly the Variétés-Amusantes) in Paris. It portrays the shipwreck of a group of squabbling European royalty plus the Pope and the Russian Czarina on a small volcanic island, and culminates in their death when the volcano erupts. The play was met with wild enthusiasm both by audiences and the radical press as "a fit spectacle for republican eyes" (Hébert, in Carlson, 177 and Root-Bernstein, 222). It was strongly supported by the government, which donated gunpowder to be exploded at the end of each performance (Carlson, 177) and paid for several thousand copies to be distributed throughout the country (Rodwell, 165). Thus in defending the Revolution against the coalition of European powers determined to destroy it, Maréchal's play seemed, and for the moment was, perfectly in tune with the spirit of its time and the will of both people and government.

But an abrupt turn was about to take place and a new strategy would be implemented in short order. The dechristianization campaign, led by radicals to the left of the government, constituted a potential power base for rivals. Also, to get rid of religion meant getting rid of what most intellectuals and politicians of the time saw as a necessary restraint on popular emotions as well as a powerful force for national unity, especially among the still-devout French peasantry. Moreover, France's international reputation as an atheistic country could turn populations in allied countries (Switzerland and the United States) against what might be interpreted as barbaric excess; for hostile countries, meanwhile, Robespierre was always careful to insert a wedge between populations and rulers. He thus effected a surprising turn. The dechristianization campaign – always scattered and uneven – was ended and its leaders imprisoned; Maréchal's play was taken off the stage in February 1794 after twenty-two successful performances (Kennedy et al., 4); parody of Catholic ritual, a staple of revolutionary theater, was now forbidden. On May 7, 1794, Robespierre's report to the Convention proposed a new official policy. No longer was atheism a respectable intellectual option, but now a counter-revolutionary offense, a disguise for provocative and treasonous behavior leading to civil war and demoralization and "lié à un système de conspiration contre la République" ("linked to systematic conspiracy against the Republic": Robespierre, 7). The Convention was asked to declare that "le peuple français reconnaît l'Être Suprême et l'Immortalité de l'âme" ("the French people acknowledge the Supreme Being and the Immortality of the soul"). Robespierre proposed a new Festival of the Supreme Being (as well as thirty-six other ten-day festivals, for which Maréchal, perhaps surprisingly, composed hymns). This took place on June 8, 1794, celebrated with all due pomp, ceremony and expense (cf. Ozouf, chap. 5), designed and supervised by the pro-revolutionary painter Jacques-Louis David. It was a conciliatory effort that radical revolutionaries must have viewed with dismay as an ignominious concession and retreat. Given Robespierre's sharp warning to influential literary men, it was doubtless lucky for Sylvain that the *Révolutions de Paris* had published its last issue in February 1794.

In this new scenario it is scarcely surprising that the subversive *Nouvelle légende dorée* could neither thrive nor come to further printings.

INTRODUCTION

Truth to tell, even during its two- to three-year history before 1793, it was no bestseller; readers preferred novels and amusing fare (Hesse, 4), and even Maréchal's good friend, the atheist astronomer Jérôme Lalande, omitted it from his obituary essay and bibliography. An early scholar referred to it as "livre rarissime, inconnu aux principaux biographes" ("an extremely rare book, unknown to the main biographers"), and although no longer unknown it has been dismissed with few and unflattering words.[7] Could Maréchal have hoped or expected otherwise? Was it pointless, mere tilting at windmills, to try to win the French reader, especially the devout woman reader, away from Catholic values and for those of the Revolution?

I think not, for two reasons. One is that the current of revolutionary thought in the first couple of years, 1789–1790, looked promising in this respect because of anti-clerical legislation (some of it mentioned above) and because of popular anti-clerical feeling, particularly in Paris. The other is that hagiography was a popular genre in city and countryside alike. Itinerant booksellers, the *colporteurs*, brought religious and secular materials into every part of the country, and literacy rates were fairly good for both men and women (Roche, 199–204); saints' lives sold well. The average person would encounter saints in many other formats as well: popular calendars and almanacs that featured a saint per day, place names and street names, the Sunday sermon, statues and shrines in churches and other public places. The lessons associated with saints and their lives would have to be confronted and rejected: humility, acceptance of persecution, above all the supervaluation of Catholic doctrine and clerical authority over the duties of family and citizenship. Two years later, during the so-called dechristianization campaign, "it was above all the saints who bore the brunt of this operation" as wood or plaster saints were smashed and gold or silver ones melted down: They have gone off to work miracles, was the popular joke (Vovelle, 55). Thus in choosing this genre as a vehicle for his ideas, Maréchal need not have meant to produce a mere rhetorical curiosity with erotic undertones; he could, not unreasonably, have hoped that his propaganda might reach a responsive audience and in some small way do its part for the Revolution, perhaps even achieve the popularity of his 1788 *Almanach*.

INTRODUCTION

That Maréchal produced an all-female legendary also suggests a genuine propagandistic impulse, for this is an unusual, though not unique, authorial choice in the history of hagiography. Most hagiographers have been men, and something like 75 per cent of saints over the centuries have also been men. To offer an all-female legendary thus skews the genre in a distinctive way, and requires explanation. In this case, I suggest that it is an issue of audience (rather than, say, of patronage or dynastic politics: Delany, *Impolitic Bodies*). Although he addresses both the male and the female reader in his text (as is clear in the gender-inflected French original), the all-female tactic makes sense as an appeal to the devout woman reader, that she might more readily relate to the lives, especially those of the married or maternal women sanctified, canonized or beatified by the Church.

†

The most sharply politicized moment in Maréchal's life was not, in my view, his editorship of the *Révolutions de Paris*, important as that journal was, but rather his association with François-Noel Babeuf and the so-called conspiracy that Babeuf eventually organized and led, between 1793 and 1797. A feudal law specialist and popular legislator in the Picardy region, Babeuf both witnessed and understood the legalized oppression of peasants, artisans, and small shopkeepers. He became a leader and spokesman in their struggles against feudal taxes and restrictions, articulating in speeches and writing the widespread anger and desires of rural populations. For this reason he adopted the first name Gracchus, after the Roman brothers (about 130 BCE) who fought for agricultural reform. Babeuf established a connection with Maréchal, whose work he knew, in March 1793 (Rose, 138; Dommanget, *Sur Babeuf*, chap. 10) and they became friends and collaborators. After moving to Paris, Babeuf published his own journal, the nationally popular *Le tribun du peuple*. In 1796 the Society of Equals was formed, a rather loosely defined body of people committed to the 1793 constitution, to the overthrow of what they saw as the tyranny of the prosperous classes (who in 1794 had got rid of Robespierre and the more radical elements in the legislature), to land redistribution, and to universal education, along with other social reforms. Babeuf himself, at least according to his close friend, colleague, and belated biographer Philippe Buonarroti, had further goals that together can legitimately be considered proto-communist: an armed coup; a revolutionary state apparatus serving the needs of workers and peasants; abolition of private property; land redistribution; universal suffrage; a planned and centralized economy; the disappearance of class difference. He opposed inheritance, extreme wage differentials, and the antagonism of intellectual and manual work. But this complete program did not appear in all the group's propaganda, and many who attended meetings would not necessarily agree with all of it, not even those in its leadership. The group evidently had over 2,000 members and several thousand sympathizers including workers, soldiers, police, and professionals.

Sylvain was among the leadership of the Babeuf group, part of what we might call its Central Committee, whose job was to discuss principles, strategies, and tactics, and to prepare the uprising. His leaflets and songs expressing its views were sung and postered all over the city and the country. He wrote a "Manifesto of Equals" for the group (somewhere between 1794 and 1796), addressing the people of France. It calls not for agrarian reform but for something "plus sublime et plus équitable, le bien commun ou la communauté des biens! Plus de propriété individuelle des terres" ("more sublime and more equitable: the common good or community of goods! No more private property in land"). It envisions universal education and an end to revolting distinctions of rich and poor, master and servant, governing and governed – evidently a classless society. Nonetheless, other of its formulations caused the other committee members to table the leaflet (Dommanget, *Sur Babeuf*, 235).

What were Sylvain's own politics? He considered himself an "egalitarian": indeed this label provided the title for Maurice Dommanget's magisterial and detailed biography. But the label leaves a lot undefined, and it seems to me that if the planned coup had succeeded, Maréchal might not have been content with the Babouvian revolutionary regime either. To be sure, in his journalism Maréchal is a constant and vitriolic critic of the "new tyrants" who have hijacked the revolution; however, this critique is not in the direction of a proto-communist program but rather toward an idealized "state of nature." If we consult other works, earlier and later, we find little in common with the Babouvian model; the labels that must supplement "egalitarian" are, in my view, "anarchist" and "agrarian-utopian." He did not approve of a state, any state, however revolutionary in intent; he deplored laws, civil society, cities and international commerce despite his commitment to international revolution (yet another contradiction!); he wanted people to be organized in familial clan structures with the oldest male as patriarchal ruler. His *Correctif à la Révolution* (1793) elaborates these ideas at tiresome length.

The earlier (1791) and more interesting *Dame Nature à la barre de l'Assemblée Nationale* (*Lady Nature at the Bar of the National Assembly*) is a brilliant, bitterly impassioned denunciation of the government's newly-enacted constitution which — Sylvain's lawyerly spokeswoman maintains — has preserved all the gangrene-producing seeds of corruption: royalty, commerce with its base passions, religion with its errors, law with its subterfuges (14). Nature despises mass society, cities, and redistribution of property. She deplores its now-falsified words (e.g., *brother, nation, liberty, people*) and its pompous new rituals. In short, Maréchal deconstructs the verbal and visual semiotic of the new regime; but his solution is the same as it would be years later: "l'homme en famille isolée, propriétaire d'un champ," with a community of perhaps 100 "du même sang," leading a life of "douce médiocrité" ("man in a separate family, owner of a field," in a community "of the same blood," leading a life of "gentle/sweet mediocrity [i.e., avoiding extremes]": pp. 40, 37).

Yet if Maréchal did not share all of Babeuf's or Buonarroti's vision, he shared some of it: above all the commitment to a real social revolution — the "grande belle révolution" invoked by Dame Nature but not yet achieved, the great future revolution to which 1789 was "avant-courrière" ("forerunner"; "Manifeste"). He cared deeply about ameliorating the condition of the working masses urban and rural, a passion evident well before 1789, as is clear from even a work as apparently removed from polemic as his *Costumes civils actuels de tous les peuples connus* (*Current Local Costumes of All Known Peoples*, 1788). This beautifully illustrated survey starts with Paris, opening with a scathing, heart-wrenching visual and verbal portrait of the Paris poor. It then moves step by step up the social ladder, showing the dress typical for each class in a sharply pointed social commentary. As to colonialism and color, Maréchal welcomed the three Haitian delegates who were seated in the Convention (Aubert, 111–12). It is surely not irrelevant that one of his colleagues at *Révolutions de Paris* was L.F. Sonthonax, who, as representative of the revolutionary government in Saint-Domingue (now Haiti) abolished slavery there in 1793, even before the government officially did so.[8]

In Paris, major popular revolts against the Convention had occurred in May and October 1795; both were harshly suppressed, the second by the young general Napoleon Bonaparte. Given the people's temper, there was nothing utopian about insurrection at this moment. Meticulous plans for the uprising were, according to Buonarroti, nearly ready to be implemented when a member of the organization betrayed them to the government on May 10, 1796. It isn't entirely clear how Maréchal managed to escape arrest; Dommanget adduces evidence that the informer simply didn't know his name (Dommanget, *Sur Babeuf*, chap. 10). Babeuf, Buonarroti and several others were arrested. Buonarroti was sent into exile, and Babeuf, denied legal representation, defended himself in a magnificent speech that lasted three days; he was executed on May 27, 1797.

While Babeuf sat in prison awaiting trial, Maréchal published the most – perhaps the only – deeply poignant of his works: "L'Opinion d'un homme" ("A/One Man's Opinion"), first as an article in the *Tribun*, then as a widely distributed pamphlet. Here Maréchal bids farewell to a friend and comrade, and to his last hope, incarnated in the now obviously guillotine-bound Babeuf, of the true revolution, the one that might have offered at least the possibility of moving to genuine "liberty, equality, fraternity." After the "érudition et plaisanteries" (2) with which the piece opens, the bitterness sets in: three million people in six years have died, and there is still tyranny in France, there is still poverty and inequality. 1789 was a magnificent moment, but it lacked the leadership that Babeuf could have provided to take it to the next level (4–5). France is not ruled by virtuous men in the tradition of Lycurgus, Rousseau or the Gracchi, but by trivial, corrupt hypocrites, insects, worms in ordure. The piece not only pays homage to Babeuf and their shared, defeated vision ("ta sublime théorie"), but encourages and counsels the imprisoned leader in his approaching martyrdom.

After this tragic episode, Maréchal took up his habitual themes. Was the Babeuf interval merely, in Françoise Aubert's striking image, a parenthesis in Sylvain's life; was he lost or led astray ("égaré") by Babeuf, as François Furet patronizingly suggests (201); did the will to survive stifle a political vision? I think it is a bit more complicated than any of these: I believe that he recognized the futility of further activism or propaganda and gave up hope.

In 1797 Maréchal published the *Culte et loix d'une société d'hommes sans Dieu* (*Ritual and Laws of a Society of Men Without God*), a model for an elite club of patriarchal atheists with its own insignia, processions, and motto: "A-t-on besoin d'un dieu, quand on a la vertu?" ("Is god needed when there is virtue?") The HSD (Hommes Sans Dieu) are patriotic but apolitical (yet another Sylvain paradox); their only concern is the regeneration of morals (chaps. XC, XCI). Spinosa [sic] is mentioned as a model, but Sir Thomas More's *Utopia* seems the more relevant text. In 1800 came the *Dictionnaire des athées anciens et modernes* (*Dictionary of Ancient and Modern Atheists*), a heterogeneous compilation of some 800 names of skeptics, atheists, doubters, heretics, provocateurs and people whose words or ideas were close enough to materialism or atheism to be nearly the same thing (Lalande, 14); these included Maréchal himself, Jesus, Job, Mahomet, and Moses. The "Discours préliminaire" sketches an idyllic bygone age, much the same as that recommended a decade earlier in *Dame Nature*.

Besides the *Projet*, discussed above (which definitively put paid to the egalitarian notion of "une seule éducation" 'universal education'), 1801 saw publication of an epistolary novella, *La femme abbé*, and *Pour et contre la Bible* (*For and Against the Bible*), a book-by-book "Bible as literature" analysis of Hebrew and Christian scriptures. The novella narrates the tale of a young woman who, adoring a handsome young priest, dresses as a man to be close to him. "J'y étais autorisée par plusieurs exemples" ("I was authorized in that by several examples": p. 18), the heroine claims. Among these examples Sylvain surely had in mind the legends of Saint Marina (whose life he has included in his legendary) and Pope Joan; closer to our time, Isaac Bashevis Singer's well known story "Yentl" offers another instance of the trope. In portraying the success of young Agathe in the seminary, Maréchal has, paradoxically, to rely on exactly the rational arguments for female equality that his *Projet* attempts to refute. Her broken-hearted expiration is highly unconvincing, but was probably the only way Maréchal could avoid confronting the central issue of her successful clerical career. The novella also reprises a theme of the *Légende*: that women often entered the cloister for reasons other than faith. If for Maréchal this observation carried the negative valence of opportunism, for Caroline Bynum it is, on the contrary, a form of empowerment: "to reject unwanted marriages, to substitute religious activities for more menial duties within the family, to redirect the use of fathers' or husbands' resources, to criticize powerful secular or religious authorities, and to claim for themselves teaching, counseling and reforming roles...to tame disorderly male behavior...to escape the role of food preparer or nurturer" (220-22).

In the other publication of this same year, *Pour et contre la Bible (For and Against the Bible)*, Maréchal gives a novelistic reading of Jewish and Christian scripture, with sensitive attention to character, plot and language. But there is plenty of the old, nasty Sylvain, for the book aims to demonstrate the poor ethics and morals of both Bibles and to show, through the notion of cultural relativity, that biblical literature, far from universal, is specific to long-gone peoples and places, hence of no utility in modern times. The introductory letter to "ministres de tous les cultes" ("priests of all religions") taunts them, among many other insults and reproaches, with their failure to preserve devout kings from the "révolution politique" (p. xi); it urges them to leave the priesthood, find a job, and come over to the side of reason. There are critical observations on translation and, appended to Job, an excursus on the inadequacies of several translators.

This long work broadens the anti-religious project begun in the *Légende*, extending it into the ur-text of the Judaeo-Christian tradition. In fact, Maréchal must have had the earlier work before him when he recycled a passage from it about the Virgin Mary: suppose she had said "No" to the Holy Ghost instead of agreeing to the conception of Jesus? Then we would have had no Church, no inquisitions, no crusades, no St. Bartholomew's Day Massacre of Protestants. Drawing on a century's worth of Bible scholarship, Maréchal knew of the existence of numerous gospels, observing that the Church prudently recognizes only the four that skip unedifying details. He concludes his tour de force ("notre analyse impartial") with regrets that Jesus failed to fulfill his potential as an authoritative revolutionary leader (a sample speech is thoughtfully provided) and with commendation of Benjamin Franklin's *Science du bonhomme Richard* (*Poor Richard's Almanac*), a book which, Maréchal claims, has done more good for humanity than all books composed before or since.[9]

In 1803 Maréchal died, of natural causes, in his own bed, surrounded by friends and family. Ironically, he was given a Christian burial, though I am not sure whether he got the epitaph he had written for himself over twenty years earlier:

> Cy repose un paisible Athée.
> Il marcha toujours droit, sans regarder les cieux.
> Que sa tombe soit respectée:
> L'ami de la vertu fut l'ennemi des Dieux.
>
> Here rests a peaceful Atheist.
> He walked upright (or: straight ahead)
> Without regarding the skies (or: heaven).
> May his tomb be respected.
> The friend of virtue was enemy of the gods.

✝

When I first noticed the title of Maréchal's work, in the course of researching another, earlier, all-female legendary by Osbern Bokenham, I was intrigued. What could a text written in 1790, during the early days of the French Revolution, do with its eponymous medieval prototype, the massive thirteenth-century compilation by the Genoan Dominican bishop Jacob Voragine? Meant as a rich resource for preachers, the original "golden legend" (*Legenda aurea*) was among the most popular and enduring texts of the Middle Ages, with over a thousand manuscripts in Latin alone still extant today. The 1790 "nouvelle" version turned out to be a bold, sardonic, witty, even nasty parody of what had once been an immensely popular religious genre. Drawing on numerous treatments and documents, the new legendary profited from rationalistic efforts to cleanse the genre of its more obvious bizarreries and fictions, as scholarly clergy labored to present a more convincing image of sainthood and the Church to Catholics and to the world at large. The monumental *Acta Sanctorum* project of the Belgian Jesuits (called the Bollandists after their early editor Jean Bolland, d. 1665) was one of these efforts. As a librarian at the prestigious Mazarin Library (he had regained the job in 1789, thanks to his support of the revolution), Maréchal would have had access to a wealth of hagiographical and related materials, many of which he quotes in his *Légende*.

But Maréchal's "nouvelle" strategy differed fundamentally from that of his intellectual hero, Jean-Jacques Rousseau. *Julie, ou la nouvelle Héloïse* (1761) borrowed epistolary form and a tutor-pupil love-story from the recently published correspondence of the twelfth-century couple Héloïse and Abelard. But little else of their gritty, tempestuous relationship surfaces in Rousseau's well-behaved (if occasionally melodramatic) novel of upper class love, marriage, and family life. Maréchal did far more: he entered into the spirit of his appropriated genre, in order to negate all it stood for and indeed all it had been devised, over a millennium earlier, to accomplish in the way of religious indoctrination. His was, instead, an attempt at de-indoctrination, a tool for unlearning and countering a thousand-year tradition of religious propaganda in its deconstruction of the Catholic master-narrative. In this sense he offers what Amos Funkenstein calls "counter-history": "a specific genre of history...[whose] function is polemical. [Its] method consists of the systematic exploitation of the adversary's most trusted sources against their grain...[Its] aim is the distortion of the adversary's self-image, of his identity, through the deconstruction of his memory"; it replaces the adversary's positive self-image "with a pejorative counter-image" (*Perceptions*, chap. 2: 36, 48). Thus, instead of a calm gallery of pious women we find a procession of crypto-lesbians, opportunists, masochists, coerced daughters, disloyal wives and mothers, unruly or disrespectful citizens together with their clerical lovers, brutal husbands, and abandoned children. Carla Hesse evokes recent interpretations of the Revolution that see it "reworking...public modes of representation and systems of signification" (*Publishing*, 2). This is what Maréchal had done in his *Livre échappé* and his *Almanach*, the books that cost him his job and his liberty (though both were eventually regained); I propose that it is what he intended in his legendary as well.

Maréchal was working within rhetorical as well as genre tradition with his satirical legendary. "Religious texts are ideal for satire," he wrote in his 1801 Bible study, and he knew whereof he spoke, for satire, parody and burlesque of religious doctrine, ritual and discourse had been for centuries well known to the French public. The Catholic Church was often able to co-opt subversion by allowing it; hence the parody feasts of the Boy Bishop or of the Ass during the high Middle Ages; the long tradition of Latin poems parodying scriptural or liturgical texts; the "sermon joyeuse" and mock hagiography; the scores of facetious saints – such as Ste. Andouille (sausage), St. Faineante (do-nothing), or St. Greluchon (lover) – exhaustively documented by Jacques Merceron. More recently, Voltaire, Diderot and other Enlightenment scholars had ridiculed or satirized the Bible; Voltaire's comparison of hagiography to *The Thousand and One Nights* had become a rationalists' trope.

As befits an erudite author steeped in ancient classics and modern literature, Maréchal drew on a variety of critical strategies and rhetorical techniques to accomplish his satirical and deconstructive aim. Foremost among them, and certainly the one most noticed and disliked by earlier scholars, is his discernment of an erotic subtext in many of the lives – an approach recently taken up by some historians of religion (e.g., Boswell, Burrus). Whether heterosexual, lesbian, or sado-masochistic, whether stated outright or conveyed by broad hints, the erotic dimension functions for Maréchal to counteract the traditional notion of asexual holiness. We need to remember, too, that sexual abuse by clergy, whether consensual or not, was a well known phenomenon of the period, so that bringing to light the possible misbehavior of saints reinforced the revolutionary demand for Church reform.

Another of Maréchal's tactics is the attribution of apparent devotion to natural causes, especially to diseases such as hysteria, madness, or "vapors" – an imbalance of humors rising to the brain to cause depression or anxiety. Opportunistic motives, as mentioned above, also serve to undercut traditional ideas about what causes women to join convents.

Making fun of some conventions of the genre is another technique, so that, for example, rather than the traditional allegorization of the saint's name that opens many traditional lives, here we are given mocking commentary on silly-sounding names or on names whose literal meaning might be construed as inappropriate to a saint. Other techniques abound. The monotony of the genre is duly noted in many places; the reader is often addressed directly and invited or urged to take a position on the narrative events; there is sarcastic hyperbolic praise for the Church; there is much double-entendre, and there are frequent wisecracks. Many of these devices amount to what the early twentieth-century Russian critic Viktor Shklovsky might have characterized as "making strange" the hitherto familiar (estrangement, defamiliarization) or what Bertolt Brecht, following Shklovsky, would go on to call "alienation" (A-effect): making it impossible for the reader simply to accept or be caught up in the work emotionally, but instead forcing the reader to evaluate and judge.

The critical reception (such as it is) of Maréchal's book makes it clear that many readers will find it offensive. I saw this contrarian, deconstructive appropriation of a medieval genre as a phenomenon important for us – not only medievalists – to understand as an example of the extension of medieval literature and ideas into the modern period, and as a special instance of hagiography: what I've elsewhere called the "afterlife" of a medieval genre (Delany, *Impolitic Bodies* and "Afterlife"). The image of "afterlife" is slightly exaggerated, for in important ways the Middle Ages wasn't entirely over when the French Revolution began. A central task that delegates to the new National Assembly set themselves was to end or at least manage the two major institutional legacies of the Middle Ages: the feudal system and the Catholic Church. Medieval chateaux were still occupied by families ennobled in medieval times, and the peasantry still lived and labored under feudal obligations and proscriptions. In August 1789, feudalism was formally abolished, though "le projet féodal" as a whole took much longer to dismantle. The absolute monarch, figurehead of the system, ruled as a constitutional monarch for three years before the Republic was proclaimed on September 22, 1792. As for the Catholic Church, the mainstream revolutionaries' impulse was to purge its obvious corruption and render it a constitutional, national church, loyal to "loi et roi." Thus when Maréchal's legendary appeared, the social-institutional context made both the medieval genre and its specific Maréchalian treatment equally appropriate.

In the fifteenth century, Osbern Bokenham produced an all-female legendary to support his Yorkist sympathies during England's dynastic debates, and used the genre additionally to mount an Augustinian critique of courtly poetry. Maréchal took a big step further — perhaps the last possible step — by turning the legendary against itself. This struck me as a meaningful moment for medievalists and literary historians to acknowledge, along with historians of religion and gender-studies specialists interested in the literary representation of women and in the address of a male author to a mixed audience at a time when the role and rights of women were sharply at issue.

I write this at a moment when religion has penetrated North American public life to an unprecedented (and to some, an alarming) degree. I thought Maréchal's work a valuable entrant in the public conversation. For me personally, it's gratifying to be in accord with Lenin's observation in his 1905 article "Socialism and religion": "We shall now probably have to follow the advice Engels once gave to the German Socialists: to translate and widely disseminate the eighteenth-century literature of the French Enlightenment and atheism." Some will want to make the banal and incontrovertible observation that it is no longer 1905. But if the Middle Ages wasn't entirely over in 1789, then we may need to think the possibility that the French Revolution isn't, either — or, if over, not necessarily complete.

NOTES

1. Dommanget (*Sylvain Maréchal*) also notes Maréchal's distinctive style, although citing different features than I have done. The article I cite is not listed in Dommanget's bibliography, as he has Maréchal's editorship beginning a few weeks later; however, I think it likely that Sylvain wrote for the journal before being officially appointed an editor. Accents and spelling as in original. In eighteenth-century publishing these were not always as consistent as they are today.

2. Others have noted the representative quality of the contradictions in Sylvain's thought, though not necessarily the same ones as I indicate, nor the same as one another's; cf. Fusil (vii–viii), Perrot (98-99).
3. The women's clubs were banned at the end of October 1793, after a series of other decrees against women's political activity and the arrest of several important women leaders.
4. I don't mean to imply here that there were earlier laws forbidding women to read; rather that earlier periods had less female literacy than existed during Maréchal's time. There have always been literate women and writing women, if frequently exceptions.
5. An expanded and retitled version of this text appeared some years later as *Le Lucrèce français* (*The French Lucretius*), named after the first-century Latin materialist poet.
6. The 1793 constitution guaranteed private property; it provided for universal education, work and relief for the poor, and some level of popular legislative power. It was suspended by the government nominally because of war on several fronts; but after the government was ousted, no new one brought back this constitution even when the wars were over.
7. The quotation is from Jules Gay, cited in Karmin, 266 and in Dommanget, 454. More recent Sylvain scholars have been typically embarrassed by the *Légende*. Fusil gave it a page (the pages of his book are very small) with the snide comment that "Il fallait soulever le coin de la tapisserie. Laissons-la retomber.... C'est par cette littérature de club et de bouge que Sylvain Maréchal travaillait à chasser le mauvais air des croisades et des cathédrales gothiques" ("A corner of the curtain had to be lifted. Let us drop it again....It's with this literature of club and dive that SM worked to get rid of the stench of the crusades and the gothic cathedrals": 70-71). Dommanget has a short paragraph coyly noting "plaisanteries qu'on devine" and "ces traits communs à l'amour mystique et à l'amour charnel qui n'échappent point à Maréchal" ("jokes that one may guess...those features shared by mystical love and carnal love that did not escape Maréchal": 165). Aubert neither mentions nor lists the book, nor does Perrot.

8. To be sure, there was also a colonial motive: abolition would strengthen loyalty to France rather than to England or Spain, which were competing with France for influence in the Caribbean and North America. However, Sonthonax was personally and politically committed to abolition; he worked in the Société des amis des noirs (Society of Friends of Blacks) and wrote defending the rights of people of color. In 1802 Napoleon sent a large army to re-establish slavery in the colonies and end the independence of Haiti, but this campaign ended in defeat for the French.

9. As a printer, scientist, political leader and writer, Franklin was a hero to French revolutionists; his invention of the lightning rod showed that humanity could use nature to its own benefit by the exercise of rational thought. Robespierre referred to this in his long 1794 speech on morals and religion: "L'homme a conquis la foudre et conjuré celle du ciel" (Man has conquered lightning and controlled that of heaven/the skies." When Franklin died in 1790, the National Assembly took three days of mourning, and a memorial was conducted by the Parisian print-workers (*RdeP* #48:540, #57:232).

TRANSLATOR'S NOTE

The translation was done from my transcription, made at Stanford University's Special Collections library, from their copy of the original (and only) 1790 edition. There are only five copies in North America. It is a small book, in two volumes, each entitled (in capital letters) *Nouvelle légende dorée, ou Dictionnaire des saintes*. The author's full name is not given; instead, another line explains: "Mis au jour par S.M. Rédacteur de *l'Almanach des honnêtes Gens*" – Maréchal's 1788 compilation that won him fame, fortune and a short prison sentence. As is frequently the case with eighteenth-century books of a controversial nature, the real place of publication – perhaps Brussels (Karmin, 266) – is disguised: in this case, ironically, as "Rome," headquarters of world Catholicism, followed with Maréchal's own home street in Paris, "Rue des Prêcheurs."

Maréchal's style in the *Légende* veers between a floridly pompous, mock-scholarly parody of the language of his sources and a deliberately casual, colloquial style meant to demystify the material and express disdain for all things ecclesiastical (e.g., his use of the abbreviation "J.C." for Jesus Christ). I've maintained as much as possible of both, and of his own rhetorical flair as expressed in wordplay, metaphor, quotations, interjected comments, and the idioms with which he spices his narratives and his interjected comments. Where a French word has two or more related and relevant meanings, I've supplied both.

Saints' names have been given English spelling for the most part; an occasional name is out of alphabetical order and I have left it. There is in the original no K section, no Q, no W or X, and U is included with and as V. I have combined I and J. I have retained minor authorial inconsistencies such as the occasional use of *N.B.* for *Nota bene* ("Observe closely"). In quotations of French texts, I have retained original spelling, while regularizing spacing (e.g., closing up spaces between words and punctuation marks). The explanatory notes are not in the original but have been added by me.

ANTI-

SAINTS

DEDICATORY EPISTLE,
WHICH CAN SERVE AS PREFACE,
WARNING, NOTIFICATION, ETC.

MY DEAR PASTOR,

God is the author of good intentions; *thus begins the dedicatory epistle of my grand-uncle, Adrien Baillet, to the Cardinal de Noailles.*[1] *I may, without vanity, appropriate this beginning for myself.* Yes, to be sure; God is the author of good intentions, since it is he who inspired this one. I may flatter myself on that score with more reason than my grand-uncle. For you know, MY DEAR PASTOR, that one of your predecessors called my grand-uncle "the great displacer of saints";[2] his grand-nephew, on the contrary, has reassembled, as best he could, some of those saints. Everywhere I have sniffed out saints and martyrs, to place them in my legendary. If you have a nice niece or a governess and had you permitted it, MY DEAR PASTOR, she would have enlarged the list of my saints. Perhaps I wouldn't have been able to place her among the virgins, but one way or another I would have managed to classify her. Bless therefore my labor.

This work was needed. Every time I attend the announcements at the end of your mass (and I attend no more than a dozen times a year, since you don't do it more than once a month), your audience is composed only of nuns' headdresses; whence I conclude that, without women, there would be no more faith in Israel.[3] Emulation is the mother of virtues, so I say on my own behalf that although my grand-uncle Adrien Baillet compiled the lives of men and women saints, nonetheless could a religious woman, even with two big lackeys to carry her purse and her train, walk with my grand-uncle's four huge folio volumes? Thus I decided to reduce them into a little pocket-size volume. If he returned to the world, he wouldn't feel any the worse about it.

I am going to give you an account of my work. I have made it my law to be true.

I have attached myself only to the most edifying features of each saint. To appreciate my enterprise, it's necessary to confront the nephew with the uncle.

My grand-uncle speaks all the time; his nephew is often silent... ...But let us not disturb the ashes of the dead.

So I hope, *MY DEAR PASTOR*, *that you might, in your announcements, recommend the reading of our legendary; that you will exhort every mother of a family to have a copy of it in her house, and every night to have her eldest daughter read her a saint's life.*

You might also recommend me to all the religious convents; this book should enter into the classic works destined for religious communities. The author, for his salary, limits himself to the kindness of his readers and to the benediction of his Pastor.

The grand-nephew OF ADRIEN BAILLET, on the female side.

A

Saint ACCIE, wife of Saint Genitor. Genitor!...Odd name for the husband of a saint!...Accie, who is sometimes named Accia-Claudia, died about 252, leaving her son St. Genou. The nomenclature of this holy family is amusing.[1] See the "Antiquities" of Berry.[2]

The Blessed ADELAIDE, queen of Italy, then empress of Germany. This princess was, as far as she could be, the benefactress of the Church: too unlucky, she did for religion as much good as is necessary to be declared blessed, but not enough to become a saint.[3]

Saints AFRA, or SAFRA, and her companions, HILARY, her mother, DIGNE, [and] EUNOMIE [and] EUTROPIE her servants, [all] martyrs. The holy Bishop Narcissus, chased out of his country, comes to Ausbourg with Felix, his deacon; he enters Afra's home, "without knowing her," they say; now Afra or Safra was a "public" courtesan. They were well received; they sat at table, passed the night with chanting, etc. and Safra is converted. The morning of the next day, people come to seize the holy bishop. (Today they are more prudent.) Afra suffers martyrdom, but her catechist runs off.

Saints AGAPE, CHIONIA and IRENE, sisters, and their companions, martyrs. We will make a necessary observation here. Is it believable that grave Roman magistrates had the ferocity to invent unheard-of punishments for young girls who ought to be inspired by other sentiments than that of indignation; and all that to punish them for their vapors,[4] for their brains exalted by obscure fanatics? However, this is what the legend says happened to our three martyrs and to an infinity of others.

To speak more particularly of these, the first two were, they say, burnt alive without preliminary. For the third, Saint Irene, it's said that she remained intact, exposed nude for several days to the view and the free desires of the entire debauched youth of Thessalonica in Macedonia. They add that the same saint, preserved by the grace of the Holy Spirit from the injuries to which her virginity was condemned, could not be saved from the burning pyre onto which they forced her to throw herself. It is easy to respond to this captious objection. It's that apparently, a virginity is more precious in the eyes of the Lord than a life.

Saint AGATHA, virgin and martyr. Agatha was beautiful. Quintian, governor of Sicily, was taken with her and pursued her under the pretext that she was Christian. We can be sure that the proconsul was rather gauche, or was little accustomed to worldly life. To seduce this untamed but not untamable virgin, he used strange ways. It isn't by the mediation of officious and vile women; it isn't by atrocious torments that one can bend an innocent and therefore weak girl. It isn't by ripping the breast of a maiden that one succeeds in making it palpitate with love; and we believe we would offend the penetration of our readers if we outlined here the conduct that the inept governor should have held to. Our intendants[5] from the provinces know all about it.

Nonetheless we fear we might have made a somewhat too severe judgment of this Quintian; for we have read in a corner of our heroine's life that she healed almost immediately from the "profound wounds" that her persecutor inflicted. They add, true enough, that Agatha succumbed then to the many blows she was given, and obtained the palm of martyrdom along with the crown of virginity.

Saint AGLAE and Saint Boniface. She was a foreign woman who lived in Rome toward the beginning of the fourth century. She had as manager of her wealth one Boniface who was also manager of her pleasures. After having lived together what is called a joyous life, distaste seized them and made of the manager a martyr and a saint of his mistress.

Saint AGNES, virgin and martyr. Agnes had barely begun to be nubile when she married J.C. But as this spouse was invisible and without a body, and as Agnes was beautiful, the best-looking boys in Rome hastened to try to be the visible and carnal spouse of this saint, who could choose among them without offending her divine husband. J.C. could have had the soul, and one of the inhabitants of Rome could have had the rest. This arrangement wouldn't have been absurd and would have avoided many scandalous scenes.

This virgin, closing her ears to honest proposals from several presentable parties, made enemies who wanted to put to a rude test the rights of this celestial spouse into whose arms Agnes always threw herself. Not wanting to sacrifice herself on the altar of the wise Pallas, she was led to that of Priapus.[6] Agnes's husband was evidently jealous and resembled the dog in the fable, who, bedded on a heap of straw from which he couldn't benefit, drove away the hungry cattle with his barking. Thus Agnes (if we must believe the legend, and we know how believable it is) left the temple of voluptuousness just as she had entered it, and everyone cried miracle; assuredly it was one.

Meanwhile they add that there Agnes recalled to life a young man who, at first, seemed to her "scarcely frightening." Again they cried miracle. But here we will take the liberty of observing that this second deed is not as supernatural as the first. We will also admit, with the impartiality we profess, that when the judge offered Agnes the alternative of the altars of Diana or those of Priapus, our saint could have chosen the first rather than consenting to be led to the second. No doubt the god had made her feel his power. Agnes had her head cut off and went to join her celestial spouse, who could have saved her the cost of the trip.

We have sought in vain the reason that gives the name of this saint to all inexperienced young girls, who are not as Agnes as their patron saint.

The Blessed AGNES, sister of Saint Claire. She was the younger sister of Claire and imitated her elder sister all too well. She left, like her, the paternal home; like her, she preferred to the duties of a tender daughter those of a nun and was rewarded for this by beatification. If I were a mother, Agnes would not be the patron saint of my daughters.

The Blessed AGNES of Bohemia. Daughter of the first king of Hungary, Agnes made herself a religious of Saint Claire. That happened in 1283; in 1789 it would have happened differently.[7]

Saint AGNES of Mont-Pulcien, religious in the order of Saint Dominic. Born about the year 1274 in the village of Monte-Pulliana in Tuscany, from the age of nine years she went to the Sachine sisters, thus named because of their rough-woven scapular,[8] from which they made "sacks." At fourteen years old she was named cellarer of the convent, and at fifteen was consecrated abbess. She converted a house of debauchery into a monastery of penitence. The Dominicans inherited her body: when will we be able to add "and her virtues"?

ALEINE, see MELANIE.

Saint ALDEGONDE, virgin. She was of the royal blood of France and of a family entirely holy. She vowed herself to celibacy, for they believed then that there was no other way to please God, who expressly recommended that humanity should multiply. Aldegonde placed herself at the head of several holy girls like herself. Envious people loudly blamed the society of this recluse and her companions, which they didn't believe as innocent as it doubtless was. Aldegonde died of a cancer that devoured her breast: the breast which, according to the profane, was not given to her to be tormented under a penitential shirt.[9]

Saint ALEXANDRIA, see Saint CLAUDE or the seven octogenarian virgins of Ancyra.

Saint ALODIE, see Saint NUNILLON.

Saint AMALBERGE, twice a widow and mother of three saints. This holy woman, after having had a half-dozen children from two husbands, believed that it was time to take Jesus Christ for a third husband. The latter, far from being as fecund as his predecessors, on the contrary brought our widow to consecrate all her children to him and at one blow to extinguish six acts of generation. Such a fine feature merited canonization for Amalberge.

Saint AME or AMEE or EMMA or YMME, see Saint LINDRU, her sister.

Saint AMALBERGE, virgin and not martyr. This virgin, born in the Ardennes in 741, loved J.C. so much that she wanted absolutely no other lover, although she was beautiful. A number of sighing suitors confronted her in vain; she always asked if they resembled J.C. On the answer depended the fate of the suitors. One young man who apparently had some similarity to the one she loved "gave her such brusque and violent caresses" (these are the very expressions of the ancient legend) that he hurt her seriously, we don't know where... The holy maiden had trouble in healing, they say, and not finding the game as good as she had probably believed, she cloistered herself and died at thirty-one years. We are astonished that the Church didn't make a martyr of her.

Saint AMMONAIRE, see DENYSE, martyr of Alexandria. There are two of this name.

The Holy AMPOULE. This is not a saint. You have to be in a republic to be able to give an exact definition of the Holy Ampoule.[10]

Saint ANASTASIA, virgin and martyr. A girl of quality from Rome, she was placed, at her mother's death, in the hands of a holy priest named Chrysogon. Her father made her marry, against her will, a débauché, whose conduct toward her was a martyrdom perhaps more real than the one they say she suffered later on: for this husband didn't prevent the Church from placing his wife in the rank of virgins; beyond that, he held her prisoner in her own house. Anastasia regretted less her lost liberty than the consolations of the priest Chrysogon, who had shaped her earliest youth and had received the first fruits of her "charity." God wanted to reward this martyr spouse by removing her husband. This "ending" returned her to herself and above all to her spiritual director who, during the captivity of his pupil, had been sufficiently prudent to turn a deaf ear to the frequent missives which our saint secretly sent him. She used her liberty to follow her director to Aquilea; she paid him well. After the death of the blessed one, she resigned herself without pain to the torture by fire that they inflicted for having helped with her goods and credit, etc. the adherents of J.C., rebels to the emperors.

Saint ANATOLIA and her sister Saint VICTORIA, Roman virgins. Anatolia was going to marry. Victoria, her younger sister, irritated at going last, and cleverer than Anatolia, knew so well how to restrain her elder sister's intelligence that she made it consent to remaining a virgin. The frustrated lover avenged himself too cruelly, no doubt; or rather he only sought to frighten them by declaring them Christians. But he knew ill the human heart. That of women, weak when you agree with it, stiffens against obstacles, and vanity performs in it prodigies of love. They preferred to suffer martyrdom than to have their pride contradicted.

Saint ANGADREME, virgin, patron saint of Beauvais; in Latin, ANGADRISMA or ANDRAGISINA. Born under the reign of Clotaire III, son of Clovis II," Angadreme was the daughter of Robert, the great referendary or guardian of the king's seal. They married her off against her will to the young Ansbert, who didn't care much one way or the other. Our two spouses, moreover, were already engaged. Angadreme had chosen Jesus as her man and Ansbert the Church as his wife. So our two newlyweds didn't dare be unfaithful. Furthermore, they add (and we wouldn't believe it if we hadn't found it in the truthtelling legend) that the young Angadreme, who was perfectly beautiful, prayed heaven to make her ugly; and that God, favorable to her prayer, covered her with an awful leprosy. Far from allowing herself to be cured, she made it serve as pretext to break with her carnal husband and enclose herself in a convent of which she was the mother superior and consequently a saint. It's this patron saint that the cowardly citizens of Beauvais invoked rather than take up arms to lift the siege of their city by the duke of Burgundy in 1473. But the women, more courageous and less devout, did their husbands' job and delivered their country, which probably Angadreme couldn't have done. The day of our saint's feast, the bourgeois of Beauvais make a procession where they give pride of place to their wives, in memory of this incident which the wives have no intention of forgetting.

The Blessed ANGELA of Foligno, in Umbria, widow, of the third order of Saint Francis.[12] The life of this semi-saint is filled with incomprehensible and "consequently" unbelievable things, except, however, the little infidelities against her husband that she did while he lived. Which is more believable than the twelve consecutive years that she spent with no other nourishment than the flesh of her God, which "is thin meat" whatever else might be said about it.

The Blessed ANGELA of Ditenzano, founder of the Ursulines. This one remained a virgin, it's said, although doing the work of a pilgrim. She traveled to Jerusalem, to Rome, and founded a monastery. Great!

The same article corrected:

The Blessed ANGELA MERICI, from Bresse in Lombardy, first founder of the Ursulines. This Lombard saint lived in the good old times.[13] At the beginning of the sixteenth century, it was still the fashion to found convents. Only one or two miracles are mentioned in her entire life, without counting that of the incorruptibility of her body for a long time after her passing. Heaven owes this favor to someone who never soiled her baptismal dress.

Saint ANNE, claimed mother of the Holy Virgin [Mary], or Saint ANE.[14]

Let the benevolent reader permit this reflection! The Greeks and Romans were assiduous in giving harmonious names to their divinized heroes. Even the god Fart, Crepitus in Latin, is a sonorous word and has an imitative harmony (onomatopoeia) to practised ears. The Church, in reversing the cult of paganism, seems to have taken in everything the opposite step from ancient idolatry: it wanted to confound the pride of scholars, philosophers and people of taste in offering them only bizarre, barbarous and often ridiculous names – as, for example, the one borne by the claimed mother of the mother of Jesus.

And another little observation, while we're at it. But this one comes from the heart of the matter and returns to it.

There are many nobles who take their glory from a borrowed source and who would be nothing if their ancestors hadn't been something. The Church, to confound them, gives them a contrary example here. It is certain that Anne or Ane wouldn't have played a big role in the Catholic world without Mary, virgin and mother all at once; and it is more than likely that the mother only owes her altars to those of the daughter.

However, although several cities dispute the honor of possessing the corpse of Ane, although the monks of Orcamp claim to have her skull (which, parenthetically, must be pretty hard) and the Provençals her head; it is still undecided whether the saint who has the name of Ane is really and truly the mother of the mother of Jesus. Much more, it is even doubtful that she ever existed..."O! altitudo!" we would write with the apostle![15] Only God knows what it is. Saint Anne has her chapel in the village of Anières. The Carmelites celebrate her feast day, with good cause.[16]

Saint ANNE, widow, prophetess. This eighty-four-year-old widow was at the temple when Jesus was presented to old Simeon.[17] This lucky encounter bought her the honors of canonization.

ANNE, mother of Samuel, saint, in the Old Testament.[18] This was a Jewish woman who wept for someone to make a child for her. This little stratagem succeeded; she had the great Samuel. We don't produce this saint as a model for our benevolent readers to follow. If, to become mothers, they only had the resources of this holy old woman, we would doubt their fecundity, especially in this century when no one believes any longer in the tears and vapors of women.

The Blessed ANTOINETTE of Florence. The proof that Antoinette was a saint is that since the year 1272, date of her death, they have been changing her shirt every Sunday.

Saint ANTONINE. It isn't known whether she was maiden, wife, or widow. It is only certain that she was martyred. She was burnt at Byzantium, May 3, and at Nicaea, June 12, 303, unless one would rather assume two saints of the same name.

Saint AOUSTRILLE.

Saint APPOLINE or APPOLONIA. This virgin, ninety years of age, was condemned to have all her teeth broken. At ninety, this martyrdom wouldn't have been long or rigorous. They threatened her with being thrown into a nearby oven; she threw herself in, to the great astonishment even of the infidels, who didn't find this type of suicide orthodox. But religion, as is known, legitimizes everything. Everything is fine when it's about the Church's glory and above all about the interest of her ministers.

    This saint, burnt at Alexandria, is invoked at Bourges against toothache, "for they broke hers." This remark isn't from us. We found it just that way in a serious dissertation by the good Catherinot Berrichon, historiographer of his province.

Saint APPIA, virgin, wife of Saint Philemon, disciple of Saint Paul. She went to a good school! The good apostle was the friend of the husband and teacher of the wife. A little later they would have made Saint Paul submit to the Asiatic ceremony that Abelard suffered, who merited it much less.[19] But it was quite otherwise. The husband Philemon was publicly whipped and stoned; it is true that his wife Appia shared martyrdom with him. As for Paul, he went on to do his business elsewhere.

Saint APRE, virgin, daughter of Saint Hilary, bishop of Poitiers. This was a little girl who, having asked permission of "her dear father" to love, obtained from him only permission to love God.

Saint ARTONGATHE, or ERCONGOTE, see EDELBURG.

Saint ASELLE or AZELLE, Roman virgin. Aselle was among the numerous troupe of holy women whom Jerome[20] entertained at Rome. She appears to have held a distinguished place in the heart of the blessed father of the Church. When he left the capital of the Christian world, it was to her that he wrote and her to whom he most commended himself.

Saint ATHANASIA, widow, abbess of Timea in Greece. This saint, before marrying, had vapors; it isn't necessary to be a saint to have them, but it is necessary to be one in order to believe they're divinely inspired. She was married, against her will, they say, to a young officer who only spent sixteen days with her. This time didn't suffice, apparently, to cure his wife, who, finding herself widowed by the death of her husband, who was killed in the army, got ready for the monastic life.

    The emperor Michael-the-Stutterer, who needed soldiers more than saints, gave an edict to oblige nubile girls and young widows to take husbands. Athanasia was happier than she deserved. She hooked a good man with whom she did, they say, all the good works that she could have done alone: alms, prayers, and even "abstinences." She did so well that she convinced him to become a monk, and our saint converted her household to the convent. Strange metamorphosis!

    A blessed priest "cut the hair" of Athanasia and of her companions and consecrated them. The holy chronicle, which sometimes doesn't differ much from a scandalous chronicle, adds that she was accused of hypocrisy and that her "austerities" were thought to be only "temptations of the demon." She died, nonetheless, reading the psalter.

Saint AUDREY, queen of Northumberland, virgin and abbess of Ely. To be wife of two kings and remain a virgin is, no doubt, the greatest miracle of this saint. As we are not completely incredulous, we were disposed to give faith to this pious and astonishing anecdote when we discovered, in one spot in the legend, that a certain Saint Wilfrid, bishop of York, was chosen by the second husband of our saint as mediator between him and his wife, who was devoutly rebellious against conjugal duties. We were the more disturbed when, examining this fact, we learned that this same king, frustrated of his most legitimate rights, conceived violent suspicions against the queen's director, etc., etc., etc. We leave this historical point to the wisdom but above all to the discretion of our well-intentioned readers.

Saint AULAIRE or AULAYE, see Saint EULALIA of Barcelona, it's the same; or Saint EULALIA of Merida, it's still the same if you like, and so on *ad libitum*.

Saint AURA, abbess of St. Martial in Paris; in Latin, AUREA. Who has read one nun's life has read a hundred.

Saint AUREA, virgin and martyr, Spanish. This saint could be proposed as an example to weak and timorous souls in whom nature is at the level of faith. Saint Aurea hesitated at first whether to expose herself to martyrdom, in which we praise her and are not about to confuse her with those energumens,[21] those Christian bacchantes,[22] blind with a holy furor, who go to death because a foolish prejudice hides its horror from them. Fortunately, the centuries of the martyrs are for us today what heroic and fabled times were for the Greeks and Romans.

Saint AURELIA, daughter of Hugh Capet.[23] One fine morning she left her father and the court of France to go enlarge that of the bishop of Ratisbon, who ought to have sent her back after giving her, or having her given, a whipping.

Saint AURELIA, virgin, and Saint MARTANE, her mother, or MARTHA. Parents of several martyrs, by virtue of weeping on the tomb of saints they became saints in their turn.

Saint AUZEA, Benedictine. This Ause, or Auzea, had the virtue of giving paralysis to all girls bold enough to drink from her cup. When she had nothing better to do, she went into a red-hot oven, whence she emerged fresh and without a hair the less. "Essay on Monachism."[24]

Saint AUSTREBERT, abbess. From the age of ten, this premature virgin burnt with the desire to marry Jesus Christ. Her parents opposed it, as was right; also as was right, the child quit the paternal home and went to throw herself into the arms of the vicar of her divine spouse. She became an abbess and had much to suffer from her nuns, in whom nature fought, probably, grace.

Saint Omer conferred on her the veil and cut her hair with his own hand.

Saint AUSTRUDE, see OSTRU.

Saint AVOYE, see Saint HEDWIG.

Saint BABIOLA or FABIOLA, widow, Roman lady. Fabiola, or rather Babiola, had, says our grand-uncle Baillet, as her first husband a man "so vicious" that no woman in the world could have lived with him; thus she divorced him to marry another with whom she was happier.

This second husband died; not daring to take a third, Babiola attached herself to bishops, as was then the fashion among Roman ladies: witness Saints Paula and Marcella and many others. (This fashion comes back from time to time.) She traveled and rejoined St. Jerome in Bethlehem. Now Jerome was among the prelates of the Church who among us would be called a "roué." Babiola had heard an incredible story about him. Jerome, on his side, prized immensely the conversations he had with Babiola; he found in her "a quite special fervor." On returning to Rome, Babiola also took on "new arrangements with her friend Pammachus." That is the expression in the legend; Pammachus, son-in-law of Saint Paula, cousin of Saint Marcelle, and companion of Saint Jerome. She died, and Jerome, in the history he wrote of the life of Saint Babiola, entitled her "the consolation of hermits."

Saint BARBARA. Was decapitated, it is said, by her own father for not having been barbaric enough toward a certain deacon who wanted to make her a converse sister.[1]

Saint BARBARA, virgin and martyr, patron of sailors.

Saint BASSILE, Roman virgin and martyr. We can say no more than what we said in the article on Saint Pudentianne.

Saint BATILDE, queen of France and religious at Chelles. Without the too-large number of convents that she caused to be built (it was the malady of the country and the time), and without the vision of the ladder of angels, which is to be pardoned because of the frailty of the last moments of life, Batilde or Bathilde could be regarded less as a saint than as a great queen. This is why we've been tempted to take her out of the legendary; but we reflected that it was better to leave her there for the edification of the reader and to convince him[2] that one can sometimes be a saint and still do great things.

Saint BEATRIX. This virgin, sister to two saints – Saint Claire and the Blessed Agnes – couldn't fail to be one herself some day. This holy trio perhaps isn't worth the trio of the Graces.[3]

Saint BEGGE, founder of the Beguines,[4] in Brabant.

Saint BENEDICTA of Origny, Saint Romaine of Beauvais, and their companions, virgins and martyrs. These holy maidens, twelve of them, left Rome, their natal city, and, inflamed by charity, divided the Christian empire among them; each went into a different province to beg for martyrdom. The legend doesn't say what sort of martyrdom they suffered, and we will be as discreet as the legend.

Saint BERENICE, Saint DOMNINA her mother, Saint PROSDOCIA her sister, martyrs at Antioch. The infallible legend appears faulty to us here. It should have qualified these three saints as suicides since, given the alternative of losing their faith or their honor, they chose to drown themselves. Wasn't this a lack of faith?

For the rest, the reader who has heard of "the hair of Berenice"[5] is warned that this other Berenice was neither virgin, martyr, nor saint.

Saint BERTHA, widow, abbess of Blangy in Artois. Mother of five daughters and deprived of her husband, Bertha embraced the religious life. Did she do well? Did she do badly? Neither one nor the other, perhaps. But to reject the parties who presented themselves for her daughters is behavior worthy of a step-mother[6] or of a saint.

Saint BERTILLE, virgin, first abbess of Chelles in the diocese of Paris; in Latin, BERTILA. A woman used to be sure of having one of the first places in heaven when, on earth, issued from an illustrious line, she saw herself the first abbess of a monastery.

Saint BERTOARE or BERTRADE.

Saint BEUVE or BOVE or even BONNE, and Saint DODE, abbesses in Reims. Same as all abbesses, etc., see Saint OPPORTUNE.

Saint BIBIANE or VIVIANE or VIBIANE, virgin and martyr, at Rome, with her father Saint FLAVIAN, her mother Saint DAFROSE, and her sister Saint DEMETRIA, all martyrs. It costs the Church nothing to heap up mountains of martyrs, on which it places the foundations of its blood-spattered edifice.

Saint BIBLIS, see Saint BLANDINE.

Saint BIRGITTA, vulgarly Saint BRIGID, widow, of Swedish royal blood, around the year 1302. We have said somewhere in this new alphabetical legendary that the ancients knew the human heart. This assertion requires some restriction. For example, in the article on this saint, the legend reports as the first prodigy of her life, that at three years Birgitta, who couldn't put out a word up to that time, spoke, without stammering, just as clearly and easily, with as much volubility, as women of a mature age. But we see here nothing other than that Birgitta, as a saint, had to be precocious in everything; and besides, who doesn't know that all little girls of three years old begin to play at rapid and fertile babbling, which only dries up with their blood and their life?

 At ten years old, Birgitta heard a sermon on the passion of J.C. The sacred orator leaned, apparently a bit too heavily, on the disgusting details of this pious farce; so that they made such an impression on the tender brain of our young saint that she remained struck by it until her death; and this event is probably the moment and the cause of the mystical private devotion of this canonized woman. However, she didn't become unfeeling of all the sensations of nature, for at thirteen, despite her project of virginity, she submitted with rather good grace to a marriage that was proposed to her with a lord aged eighteen. She only asked that heaven bless her marriage and the children that would come of it. We like to believe that, as saint, she foresaw that she would have a fairly good number of them — and in fact she gave eight to her husband. For a saint, this fertility is edifying. Birgitta stopped at this number and from that moment went to bed separately. Good! If all the comrades of heaven had done as much on earth, the Church and the state wouldn't be any worse off for it.

Her husband died, "and" (says the legend) "Birgitta lived, by this death, her liberty augmented." After two years of widowhood, her frequent revelations and celestial visions — humanly speaking, her vapors — recommenced. There had been no question of them during her marriage. Finally, a certain canon took charge of our vaporous saint, but he didn't cure her. The sunset of her life wasn't as gay as its dawn. Birgitta only made pilgrimages and religious foundations, indeed, even mystical books. She turned the head of her daughter Catherine and died, her own head filled with pious chimeras. For a long time she was lost to society.

See the lives of the two Catherines, of Siena and of Sweden.

The Blessed BLANCHE, mother of Saint Louis,[7] tertiary. It isn't miracles that make a saint, but the third order of St. Francis hurried to put this queen in its catalog in order to have a queen and so that people would say that she died with a rope belt. Besides, she isn't the worst of their saints.

Saint BLANDINE, Saint BIBLIS, martyrs of Lyon. Only the torments that the Spanish inflicted on the Americans, Catholics on Protestants, Protestants on Catholics, Saint Dominic on the Albigensians,[8] etc. can be compared to those that Blandine and Biblis suffered, if the legend is to be believed. It stresses the details of their martyrdom with a complaisance that our readers couldn't appreciate.

Who proves too much proves nothing.

Other hagiographers say unanimously that Blandine had her throat cut at Lyon. She was a servant; they don't say if she was a servant at a cabaret. These details are, however, necessary in order to know what was Blandine's degree of sanctity. It is more difficult for a barmaid to be a saint than for a recluse who has nothing else to do. The people of Bourges go every year to visit the grotto of the Blessed Blandine.

Saint BRIGID, virgin, patron saint of Ireland. Born in the country whose patron she is, and surnamed Thaumaturge[9] because of the number of her miracles, Brigid, who was promised to J.C., refused a young man who didn't believe she was bound by that. They say that in order to be rescued from this position (not the least of the miracles in her biography), she asked and received from heaven a deformity. Liberated by this means (which strikes us as suspicious), she took three other girls with her, compatriots, left her parents and went to Media[10] in search of a bishop, the disciple of Saint Patrick. This prelate, helped by two others, received in his hands the virginity of these four holy maidens. Brigid died under their discipline.

Saint BRIGIDE or BRITTA and MAURA, virgins; in Latin, MAURA and BRITTA, from Beauvoisis and la Touraine. These twin sisters are known only through a respectable but uncertain tradition. "They tell of a candle very straight, very long, very thick, and very white throwing fire and flame during the night between the two blessed maidens." This scene ordinarily took place in a cemetery. One can judge the rest by this sample; and, as we have made for ourselves a duty of veracity (although there's nothing very realistic in the fragment that we have just faithfully quoted), we won't say more about it except that since these two sisters are saints, the Church must have had excellent reasons to canonize them.

Saint BRUNETTE. The people of Issudun go every year to a fountain with the name of this saint. It would be a way to renew the marriage at Cana.[11]

The Blessed CAMILLE, of the order of Saint Claire. Much like most nuns.

Saint CANDIDA. In the company of her husband and Pauline, her daughter, she suffered martyrdom in honor of the Trinity. She must have been tired of life!

Saint CATHERINE, virgin and martyr, at Alexandria; in Greek, ACCATERINA; in Latin, CATHARINA by corruption as if it came from the Greek *katharsis*: purification. Here's a very specific title. It would be desirable that the life of this saint were as spotless as her name. She is made out to be a virtuoso of Alexandria who went to take lessons under Origen...Origen, that doctor of the Church who armed himself with a knife and made himself a eunuch the better to instruct the Christian girls of his city. We will admit it is a strange method, but worthy of the personage who used it.

Saint CATHERINE of Boulogne, religious of Saint Claire. From the court, Catherine, aged fourteen, passed to the convent, where she had "many violent temptations." She could scarcely "hold firm against the solicitations from within and from without." Thus the chaste legend expresses it. This saint was an author. We have several works by her, of which one has as title "The Seven Spiritual Arms" and another, "The Revelations." Reading them one will learn how to kill time, how to speak without being understood, how to conceal one's intent from the senses, and many other marvelous secrets.

Saint CATHERINE of Siena in Tuscany, virgin, nun of the third order of Saint Dominic. A philosopher must be impartial and indulgent, for by these two traits he is singled out. And how couldn't he be, since the Church gives him here a first-rate example?

Catherine, born at Siena in 1347, had a dyer as her father. She was the spoiled child of her family: her gaiety and lively temper caused her to be given the name "Euphrosyne." At the age of eight she made a vow of virginity. A commitment is null when contracted without knowledge of the matter, and we want to believe that such was the nature of our heroine's vow. We will see by what follows whether Catherine needs this palliative. Besides, before deciding such an important point, it would be necessary to compare the mores of her century with those of our own: it would be necessary to...this is unfinishable. Loaded with such a heavy burden (her vow of continence), she entered the order of Saint Dominic; we admit she could have chosen a shelter more suitable to keeping her promise; but one isn't a saint for nothing. "To conquer without peril is to triumph without glory": Corneille.

The Church, during its adolescence and youth, says nothing particular about Catherine, for which we will praise its discretion. They add only that Catherine made herself commendable through her "charity." If this term isn't equivocal, at least it is honest, and Christian Rome owes many altars to the adroit inventor of this happy expression.

Thus Catherine grew in age and in "charity," in the shelter of the cloister, fastening tighter and tighter the rope belt of Saint Dominic: for Saint Francis isn't the only one who makes "use of the rope-belt." A long-winded scholar would naturally find this a place for extended discussion. But we hasten to follow Catherine to a stage more worthy of the rank we assign to her.

Meanwhile we can't keep ourselves from warning our readers that, despite "her continual pious exercises," Catherine "was attacked" (says the legend) "by a thousand indecent phantasms, by many filthy images, by temptations most shameful and most humiliating for a penitent virgin." In these disturbing moments, she had recourse to the practice of discipline, which was administered to her one by one by the monks whom the convent maintained at this community of sisters for the sake of convenience and promptitude of help. Another remarkable and exemplary thing in the life of our saint is that, for three years, she addressed and spoke only to her spiritual director.

It was also the Dominicans who wed her to Jesus and who applied to her the "stigmata" of her divine spouse. Catherine desired that the office should be done without a break, day and night. She was perpetually at prayer, in ecstasy, in verbal effusion, etc., and when some of the monks were resting, she made the others keep watch. The Dominicans, in gratitude, instituted two holidays, one for her marriage, the other for her "stigmata," which they still celebrate every year with the nuns who have followed the Blessed Catherine.

But let's come back to the place we left. Over time, Catherine acquired the greatest influence over the prelates of Rome and even the pontiffs themselves. She was their plenipotentiary. It was she who positioned and displaced them, who justified them to the princes of Europe. Charles V, called the Wise and not the Holy, resisted our saint, persisting in believing more in her judicious politicking than in her mystical writings. But we are now approaching the moment of her glory.

Gregory XI of glorious memory had excommunicated the Florentines and had withdrawn to Avignon (for the popes, who are infallible, are not therefore invulnerable) and had transferred there the holy throne of Peter the fisher. Catherine joined a certain Brigid, princess of Sweden, who married Ulson, was mother of eight little saints, and composed eight books of revelations inspired by her religious spouse, no doubt. (See BIRGITTA.)

Our two well-informed saints conceived the generous project of reconciling the pope with his enemies. This Gregory was stubborn. Obstinacy is a virtue that the throne of Saint Peter the fisher transmits fairly ordinarily to those who are seated on it. Our two nuns, in the presence of the vice-god, beg, speechify, fall to his feet and embrace them, kissing the holy slipper and wetting it with their tears. What can one do against two vestal virgins dissolving in tears and enveloped in "the fire of charity"? Gregory, softened, raises the supplicants and takes on their posture; now he himself is at their knees and the grace he promises them is doubled....

Some wicked jokers doubtless won't fail to smile, saying that our holy books are filled with similar incidents. Let us impose silence on them, crying: Useful weakness, preferable to the passive virtue of our prudes! It is through you that an entire people was reconciled with the head of Christianity! "Charity" legitimizes everything. Happy our vestal saints if, for the same price, they could always perform such great things.

Catherine received the reward worthy of her after her death. The grateful Church (with whom a benefit is never lost) has consecrated and every year celebrates her memory. Permit us, in finishing, this indispensable exhortation: Daughters of the Lord, moaning doves, who read us, learn from this example to not make rash vows prematurely. Heaven didn't heap you with its favors in order to forbid their use, especially when it's in the interest of heaven itself.

Nota bene. When they came to canonize Catherine, a rather lively dispute arose. To raise the merit of our saint, they wanted to represent her as a member of the Borghese family. Indeed, the daughter of a dyer could decently be the patron saint only of her father's guild, and would have been disdained by the well-born devout. But the Borghese family preferred its profane titles to the ignoble sanctity that others wanted to spread over their genealogy.

The Dominicans shared out the body of our saint, but those in Siena reserved for themselves "the noblest part."

Saint CATHERINE of Sweden, married virgin. From the age of seven years, Catherine loved to play: the discreet legend doesn't specify what game. But it corrects itself, for the day – or rather the night – she married Egard, the conjugal bed was the stage for a scene unheard of until then. A bloody discipline took the place of caresses for our newlyweds. Our young impious folk will ridicule this; perhaps they will even go so far as to say that a little discipline given at the right time and in an urgent case...Don't finish, you disbelieving libertines! Besides, your idea isn't new, and Catherine had a brother named Charles, who made that caustic observation before you. Catherine was then eighteen years old.

With the consent of her benign spouse, Catherine made a trip to Rome with her mother, the too-famous Saint Brigid. Habits have certainly changed. Which of our husbands today would let his pretty wife, afflicted with eighteen years, go to Rome, to modern Rome...! Nonetheless they say that after having breathed the air there for a while, boredom overwhelmed Catherine, and we want to attribute this to the separation from her husband. But her mother, a mastersaint, made a crime of this, and to punish her daughter, "had her chastised by the administration of her confessor." The reader will observe that we are only the copyists of the legend. "Catherine submitted very willingly to this pain, and finding that the remedy produced its effect, she wanted it to be continued" (the legend goes on). Good God! How mores have changed!

At this moment, death – or, better, heaven – delivered her from her husband, whose memory still troubled her despite the good offices of her director. This penitence, "thus prolonged, brought back calm to her spirit and returned to her body its youthful beauty," adds the legendary.

The young nobles of Italy, sent by the demon to tempt her, brought new worries. Brigid helped her to triumph over them. The "life of the saints" is the means she employed this second time. Her mother having died, Catherine returned to her country and enclosed herself in a convent. There was nothing to say, after a twenty-five year sojourn in Rome, but that she wanted to see it again before her death.

The Venerable Mother CATHERINE de Genes, widow, commonly CATTARINETTA, FIESCA, ADORNA, born in 1448. Nerve maladies have unusual effects; and if you believe us, they would be given the name "*malum sacrum*, the sacred illness." Nervous problems possessed Catherine at the age of twelve. A wax image representing Jesus garroted and whipped, such as is still encountered in our crossroads, was the object which developed in our young saint the germ of her illness.

At sixteen years she was married to Julian Adorno, a young noble who was nothing less than a mystic. It was not a happy household. The continual vapors of his wife, her visions, the "sweet love" with which she was devoured, began by annoying the husband and ended by embittering his character. Catherine, "to charm away her troubles," went into society a little, and society might have radically cured her; but she had a relapse in which a nun, her sister, may have played no small role. It was she, really, who nurtured the chimeras of Madame Catherine Adorno.

The nun advised Catherine to see the confessor of the local monastery. That made it worse. "Catherine" (says the legend) "was no sooner at the confessor's feet than she received in her heart a wound of divine love…in a manner so sharp that she nearly fell to the ground," and this wound was incurable. She did no more than sigh, pour out burning tears, and scream: "O! Love, I no longer desire what comes from you; I desire only you yourself." Let none of our readers decide to take all these details literally and want to put them into practice; we sincerely reproach ourselves for having been the innocent cause of the sojourn that they will be forced to make at Petites-Maisons.[1] For we will admit that the times have certainly changed.

Finally, Catherine came to a point close to imbecility. Salutary effects of grace! To this strange mania was joined a contagion that she took "while kissing the mouth of a dead woman." In a word, they didn't know what to do with our saint, when a good priest, named Catanio-Marabotti, wanted to take over her care. It was necessary (says the legend naively) that he should take direction of all her goods and worldly affairs, and he succeeded. The prudent Church is still uncertain whether to honor as a saint this vaporous woman.

We have from Catherine two mystical works in which she portrays herself with sufficient fidelity. One is a dialogue among

The soul,
The body,
Self-love,
Humanity,
The spirit,
   And
Jesus.

It is a masterpiece of pious absurdities. The other is a treatise on purgatory. To read it to the end, you have to believe.

Saint CECILIA, virgin and martyr. It's said that she condemned herself to perpetual virginity. It's said that right from the first night of her marriage, Cecilia brought her husband to continence...What don't they say about her? But can one stop with hearsay when it's about a virgin and a martyr?

Would it be for these two titles that the chaste singers in the choirs of the Opera and elsewhere have chosen this saint as their patron?

Saint CELERINE, martyr. This is the grandmother of Saint Celerine. That's all we know about her, and it's still too much for faith.

Saint CELERINE, not a martyr. This was a woman (says a doctor of theology in the Paris faculty) prompt to all sorts of good works, following her name.[2] A little pun is not inappropriate in a doctor's mouth. It's good for a theologian to humanize himself occasionally. Didn't God make himself a man?

Saint CELINE or CELINIA, virgin, at Meaux; in Latin, CELINIA or CILINIA. Celine was about to marry when Genevieve came to Meaux; her presence broke it up and the two virgins took refuge in the temple to avoid the just indignation of the young fiancé. We don't know more. But this incident is certainly not the finest in the life of the patron saint of Parisians.

The Blessed Mother JEANNE-FRANÇOISE FRÉMIOT DE CHANTAL. We will extend ourselves a bit on this saint: not because she is worth more trouble than any other, but because she is modern,[3] and most of our readers have been able to attend the ceremony of her beatification.

She was born in Dijon in 1577. Her father presided over a parliamentary court in that city. From the age of five she announced what she was to be. She got involved in all the edifying disputes that Papa Frémiot sustained with heretics. A Calvinist having given her a few candies to shut her up, the little Frémiot threw them into the fire, saying, "Look, mister, that's how the heretics will burn some day in hell": an anecdote that proves her blessed memory and the genteel education she was given.

She had a sister who, after her marriage, took our little saint to Poitou. There, they gave her as babysitter a friendly woman who tried to efface from her brain the impressions made by the catechism. This second education seemed to have some success, but the young Frémiot, faithful to her character, refused a gentleman as husband because he was Huguenot. In vain they called her small-minded and a devout imbecile; nothing could bring her around; grace was beginning to operate, no doubt. Finally, her father married her at the age of twenty to the baron de Chantal, and it was with much difficulty that she consented to prefer the running of her household to the practices of her devotion. She had six children from this marriage, of whom four survived their father, so that Mme. Frémiot de Chantal was widowed at twenty-eight, responsible for a boy and three girls.

We don't know much to say about it, but we have been impelled to notice, in reading the legendary of saints, that they have all had "violent temptations"; that is doubtless to give them more merit. However, women who live in society do not complain so much of these "suggestions of the demon," even those who are widows. The widow Chantal had so many "interior combats" to sustain that she fell unconscious from it; she also had numerous visions; and all this (as she herself ingenuously confesses) came only from the "need she had for a director, to be led in the narrow path of salvation."

Her first choice of director wasn't fortunate. The monk whom several devout women had praised to her was not to her liking. He only knew how to regulate disciplines and impose abstinences. The widow Chantal already practised fasting, so she kept him only a year. But, occupied with her salvation, she neglected everything else and allowed herself to be influenced by a servant. At last we approach the great epoch in the life of our blessed lady.

The Blessed Francis de Sales, whose friendly devotion is known, comes to preach one Lent at Dijon. Chantal devours the preacher with her eyes; he returns it; she believes she sees in him the blessed one whom she had painted for herself in her visions, the one who alone was the most suitable to direct her.

Francis soon imposes himself in the house of good Papa Frémiot, and his daughter has the happiness of speaking with him whom she had listened to so avidly. Already he has won so much territory with the widow that he comes to the point of reforming her outfits. Temptations return all the more, and it was necessary to open her heart to him who alone possessed the remedy for her cure: in a word, the bishop of Geneva made so much progress that he "saw" (says the grave and weighty historian, Marsollier)[4] "more clearly than herself into her interior; he foresaw her difficulties; he responded exactly to her needs," etc.

Friend reader, weigh well these words, especially the last ones! Notwithstanding the four vows that she had had the kindness to make to her previous director, one of which was never to leave him, Francis carried her off. Chantal begged him to confess her. "He refused at first, to test her; then he gave in to her desires...A profound peace followed the first act." (The reader, once and for all, will note that everything we quote is copied faithfully from the legendary.) But the holy bishop, who knew the heart of women, sharpened the desires of Madame de Chantal with new refusals to take charge of her. Besides, he was the "enemy of ardors." To cut it clean, and humanly speaking, the bishop of Geneva wasn't too unlike our modern French prelates; he was what is called a fop.

But already our holy widow was planning a pilgrimage to Saint Claude. She spoke of it aloud in front of Francis, so that he could respond without compromising himself nor with her compromising herself. The blessed man proposed to be there and this couldn't fail to be accepted. The more Chantal frequented Francis, the more they esteemed one another. The former director complained and wanted to shake the widow's timorous conscience, but de Sales reassured her, writing her in his own words: "Our union comes from God. God gave me to you and you to me; I am surer of it every day. Moreover, I instruct you to refer this affair to God." It was clever to have God intervene here. She consulted on the subject Father Villard, rector of the Jesuits, who said to her: "Monsieur [the bishop] of Geneva suits you; he has the spirit of the Church; and Providence wants something big from you in giving you a terrestrial seraph to guide you."

It was at the gate of Saint Claude that the great interview occurred between the saint of Dijon and the saint of Geneva. "God wants me to take charge of your conduct" (said the blessed man to his perplexed penitent). "If I have so long delayed in instructing you, I wanted to know for sure the will of God." These words were pronounced with a "holy ecstasy." The same day he received from her a "general confession," at the end of which the bishop gave her a note written with these terms: "I accept responsibility for your conduct; I will put all possible care and fidelity into it as far as my duties will allow." Nothing more energetic and more clear: they separated, no doubt satisfied with one another.

Back in Dijon, the widow's first task was to thank Our Lady of l'Étang for the success of her trip; then she wrote and signed the following vows to this virgin: "I, Frémiot de Chantal...make a vow... of obedience between the hands of my lord of Geneva. May it please him to accept this holocaust sacrifice in the odor of sweetness, and may it please him to give me grace abounding. Amen." She sent a copy of it to Geneva. De Sales didn't disapprove. He replied only: "Everything must be done by love, and nothing by force, etc." But the widow not finding in this the repose or contentment she hoped for, Francis invited her to come to the Chateau de Sales. She didn't refuse; she went, despite the infirmities of an invalid father-in-law, despite the need her children had of their mother in order to be well raised. The bishop's authority overwhelmed nature and its duties.

Once at the chateau, "the charitable prelate gave her all the time she asked"; she made him "a second general confession and renewed between his hands the vows" above. "This trip was the moment of her tranquility." The holy bishop, to achieve it, had given her among other rules this one, which was to liberate her: "Scruples banish feeling and sweetness. I could name you" (said he to his docile penitent) "rigorous people who have become libertines only because of having been scrupulous." A new morality, and Father Girard was careful to put it into practice while directing the young and timid Cadière.[5]

Francis also recommended frequent discipline to Chantal. She went another year without seeing her dear director and was very bored with life, when he asked her to come to Annecy; this was to communicate to her the project he had conceived to create a "foundation of the order of the visitation." There were great difficulties; however, she "saw" (these are her own terms) "a total necessity that this vine be planted in the vineyard of its blessed founder so that his careful hand could cultivate it." Francis was poor but Chantal was rich. The bishop of Geneva saw nothing more feasible than to found a retreat near his own region, where he could raise the Lord's sheep. "I see you" (he wrote to the widow), "I see you as a vigorous heart that loves ardently, and I am very grateful to it!" "Yes" (responded she), "yes my lord! Without if, without but, without exceptions, your will be done in father, in children, in everything and in myself." How edifying this epistolary exchange, how human!

In 1607 she renewed her vows in these terms: "I want to live forever in obedience to the divine will, to which I consecrate myself absolutely and without reserve, to obey it in the person of my lord of Geneva; with all my heart I give myself to him. Amen."

Separated once again from her dear director, she was asked to marry a wealthy young lord. We admit, with our usual impartiality, that our widowed saint had the weakness to allow herself to be tempted by these propositions. But her prior promises, which she had sealed with her blood, prevailed; and, so as to be no longer exposed to such relapses, she undertook the business, the great business, of her religious retreat. "Ah!" remonstrated the good president her father, "let me die before you abandon me." Any other woman than our widow would have dissolved in tears at these paternal urgings; Madame de Chantal, whom grace hardened amazingly, answered only a word, but this word struck home: she said that "my lord of Geneva ordered it." "It must be admitted," replied the poor president, "that this lord of Geneva has the spirit of God."

However, this too-good father wanted to speak with the Genevan bishop before settling anything. Our saint's brother was not of the same mind. "But," as Abbé Marsollier well says, "to a brother one speaks more freely than to a father," and that's what our widow did, always covering herself with the name of the great bishop of the Genevans. The interview between the relatives and the blessed man turned out as Madame de Chantal wished. The president wanted the new monastery to be established at Dijon, to be near his too-much-loved daughter. The brother (an archbishop) wanted it at Autun or Bourges, for the good of the children; but their holy mother had set her eyes on Annecy, to be closer for borrowing light from her teacher, who supported this sentiment and who, as usual, won out.

Finally we come to the most brilliant moment of our holy widow's life. She is about to enclose herself in the cloister that she has had built. Daughter and mother, the grace of heaven exempts her from the duties attached to these titles that are so sacred elsewhere, and it will close her heart forever to the cries of nature. Sacredly stepmother, piously cruel, the widow Frémiot de Chantal sees with a dry eye the tears of her aged father and, without a glance, steps over the body of her son stretched out on the doorstep of the home they were all born in, to try to prevent her leaving. Humanly speaking, we will confess that this scene horrifies us in the telling, and it is shameful for humanity to see, in this intelligent and tolerant century, incense burn on the altars raised to the memory of an ungrateful daughter and a barbaric mother. Let us cry with the apostle: "O altitudo!"

Nevertheless the historian adds that our saint had some remorse for this: we are irritated that we can't believe it because of this prayer to God which we are assured Chantal pronounced upon entering her convent: "If my parents and my children should die, it would not matter to me; my sole interest is to please God." Let us write with Lucretius: "*Tantum religio potuit suadere...!*"[6] The holy bishop of Geneva gave his benediction to the recluse widow and her companions; he cut their hair and later "visited and examined them, which he did regularly every evening." Meanwhile the good president and his wife died of grief shortly after the religious commitment of their daughter, who "needed all the resources of Francis" to be consoled for this loss, which she imputed to herself, no doubt with some basis. It was then that the bishop of Geneva occupied himself with preparing the constitution of the institution they had erected. He also continued to regulate all the business of the widow nun, who did nothing without his orders.

There is an end to everything, and the death of Francis de Sales put an end to the happiness of the Blessed Chantal. She consoled herself as best she could in assembling the memoirs of the life of her dear deceased and in demanding his canonization. She also tried to distract herself with numerous comings and goings, new foundations, etc. Meanwhile, the body of Francis began to exude the odor of sanctity.[7] After ten years they disinterred him, in the presence of his illustrious penitent. Brought to the sacristy, she "covered him with kisses," caressed all his limbs that were so perfectly preserved that one of them extended by itself, became flexible and went to the lips of Madame de Chantal who was in ecstasy, and gave her a thousand unequivocal proofs of life and feeling. This was the first of all the prodigies performed by the body of Saint Francis de Sales in the presence of Saint Chantal.

Saints are subject to death just like profane women. Chantal, feeling herself close to joining her terrestrial guide, confessed and "asked pardon, aloud, for the bad examples she had given to the community." The deathbed is always the seat of truth...She had someone read her a few chapters of the book by her blessed director, entitled "On Divine Love." She also had brought to her the mitre[8] of that saint, which she "kissed tenderly," and died. She was so humble that she had said, a few seconds earlier, that "her heart, for her infidelities, deserved more to be thrown into the sewer than to be preserved." This confession came a bit late.

Tender souls who read me, it doubtless isn't necessary to warn you that in exposing you to the life of this modern saint, our intention hasn't completely been to propose her to you as a model to follow. Believe us: while awaiting the moment of grace, continue to let yourself be guided by the hand of kindly, wise nature, which is just as good. You won't have incense after your death, but during your life you will have our respect and our love.

We are fortunate to possess the little iron chain which passed back and forth between the back of the Blessed Francis de Sales and the haunches of the Blessed Frémiot de Chantal; it served them to give each other discipline. A wicked joker[9] didn't fear to profane this relic in attaching to it these four lines:

Ridiculous instrument of devout fervor
Which Francis and Chantal who walked in his tracks
Wore by turns: belt of pain,
How ill you replace the belt of the graces.

Saint CHARITY, see Saint FAITH and Saint HOPE.

Saint CHIONIA, see AGAPE.

Saint CHRISTIANNE. Slave in Iberia, beyond Pont-Euxin, she is proposed to all good Christian women as a model in adversity. Religion sends us far off to look for examples.

Saint CHRISTINE, virgin and martyr. This saint, who had her tongue cut out, made much less noise and doubtless deserved less to do so than the famous queen of Sweden, whose patron saint she was, and who was neither virgin nor martyr.

Saint CILINIA, mother of Saint Remy. "Saint in herself and saint in her fruit," says a legendary.

Saint CLAIRE, virgin, and mother of the nuns of Saint Francis. In 1173, Claire was born at Assisi, country of the great Saint Francis of that name. At the age of seventeen, accompanied by a confidante, after several other holy pilgrimages she visited her blessed compatriot at the monastery of Portiuncula. We will observe in passing that this name is quite modest for a convent of monks.[10]

Francis received Claire with kindness. Claire immediately "opened her heart" to Francis. The blessed man found there a great store of "charity" and undertook to cultivate it. To do so, he confirmed her in her resolution to consecrate her virginity to him. It was in "their frequent conversations" that the raggedy-monk saint put it into the head of the holy nun to establish a community of nuns which would be hers as well. Claire consented to it. They had the ceremony with all the pomp worthy of the subject. Saint Francis, leading his men, who each carried a fine lit candle, received Claire in the little church of Our Lady of the Angels. He cut her hair himself and fastened about her the famous rope belt of Saint Francis. From this moment he took charge of her, despite the just murmurs of the parents of the young saint, who was only eighteen at the time.

Friend reader, don't be surprised to see us so scrupulous in citing dates. They shed light on history – and assist wonderfully in faith.

The new nuns made vows of poverty and were named the Order of Poor Ladies. From then on, they went about "presenting their mandate" to the generosity and fervor of the faithful. Claire received in her institute maids, wives, widows, even those women who were neither one nor the other. She lived long, assisted by her brother in God, Saint Francis, and died in the peace of the Church.

Nota bene. The name of this founder is a pun. Claire was thus named at baptism because she was one day to clarify or illuminate and enlighten the world. We see how the event justified the prediction.

The Blessed CLAIRE of Montefalco. After her death they opened her cadaver, and on her heart they found, distinctly marked, the imprint of a cross. That is the only noteworthy thing in the life of this blessed woman. Perhaps someone will make fun of us for having noticed her.

Saints CLAUDE, TELURE, ALEXANDRIA, PHAINE, EUPHRASIA, MATRONA, JULITTA, virgin martyrs, at Ancyra. These seven Christian virgins were condemned to be raped; or rather they condemned the young libertines of Ancyra, capital city of Galatia, to rape them. Of course they were afraid. The youngest, Saint Telure, who was seventy years old, by showing her white hair, etc., managed to repress the most intrepid desires of the executioners and to save the aged honor of her companions.

But they weren't done yet. They were stripped; and, after washing them well in a stream, persecutors promenaded them through the city. Imagine seven octogenarian virgins naked and standing on a chariot, circling a fine statue of Diana, and exposed to a whole populace which, by the permission of heaven, made no attempt on the flower of the virginity of these seven decrepit maidens. After this picturesque ceremony they attached a stone to their necks and drowned them. This ending was too much. The tavern keeper Theodotus fished out their bodies and in consequence merited the honors of martyrdom. One of the seven drowned had formerly taught the grateful Theodotus.

Saint CLOTILDE, queen of France, spouse of Clovis, first Christian king;[11] in Latin, CLOTILDIS or CHRODECHILDIS. We are pausing at only a single incident in the life of this princess. It's an answer she made, more worthy of an ancient Roman than of a saint. They send her a sword and scissors, to give her the choice of the death of her three grandsons or their tonsure. "I prefer to see my grandsons dead than to see them monks and deprived of their father's crown." We are forced to acknowledge that if heroism had its martyrology, the name of Clotilde would figure better there than in the *Golden Legend*.[12]

The Venerable Mother COLETTE, of Saint Francis, Capucine.[13] Daughter of an officer, under the name of Henrietta Catherine, and born in Paris, raised by the Ursuline nuns, Colette abandoned a father who loved only her and whose only support she was; she "silenced all the natural sentiments" (these are the actual terms of the edifying legend) "and preferred to obey God rather than men." We are astonished that the Church delayed so long in placing in its martyrology a pious girl who preferred the sacristy of a convent to the paternal home.

The Blessed COLETTE BOILET, reformer of the order of Saint Claire. Born in 1380, this holy girl was from Picardy. Her mother was sixty years old when she brought little Nicole or Colette into the world. A birth so out of the ordinary couldn't fail to herald a saint or at least a blessed person. The name they gave her came from the great devotion her parents had for Saint Nicolas, the patron saint of girls, who marries them off[14] when they are very good but who didn't get Colette married off although she was good. But if this saint disdained to become mother of a numerous posterity, it's because she had aims that were greater and more advantageous to the needs of the world. She instituted seventeen or eighteen convents for girls.

Her first step in a devout career was happy; she chose to stay at a community of Beguines, who lived as holily as one can under the spiritual direction of the Franciscan rope belt. But (says the legend) she still didn't find there what she sought. She left Saint Francis for the Cordeliers and was so pleased there that she took the habit of the third order. The reader will observe that our blessed woman was only twenty-two years old. But so far she had only made attempts. The noble desire to be a founder tormented her and made her run from cardinal to cardinal and finally to the feet or knees of the pope. From him she obtained what she wanted, reformed the "poor Claires," and exposed herself to being treated as a visionary in her region, to merit one day being invoked there as saint, which happened.

Saint COLOMBA, virgin and martyr, at Sens. That's all we know. Our readers will have all the more merit in believing in this saint.

Saint COLOMBA, virgin and martyr, at Cordova in Spain. This is again one of those young girls without experience, who, promising more than they can deliver, think they can escape nature in putting themselves under the safeguard of religion. Deep in her cell, "the demon of the flesh" (said the legend) "filled her imagination with unseemly phantasms" and cut down her spirit with depression and a frightening void. Colomba held firm, they say, and after she suffered the martyrdom of virginity, the Muslims made her a martyr of the Church. We don't know which of these two holocaust sacrifices is the less painful and the more meritorious.

The Blessed MARGUERITE COLONNA, tertiary. Born in Rome and directed by Father Bona-gratia, she became a nun at Assisi; as her brother was a cardinal, he made her a saint. Perhaps there's a bit of nepotism here.

Saint CONSORCIA, virgin. We know nothing particular about this virgin except that she was the daughter of a bishop...Let the reader, enemy to scandal, not frown! Consorcia is of the sixteenth century, and the bishops of that time had not yet acquired the right of a tax on the marriage bed of their diocesans, who could have reciprocated, for the bishops were married. Consorcia died in the odor of sanctity, and even the least instructed reader knows better than we do, perhaps, what it's necessary to have done to be a saint.

Saint CORINTHE, virgin and martyr, from Alexandria. Not everyone can get up to Corinth.[15]

Saint CRISPINA and her companions Sts. SECONDE, MAXIME, and DONATILLA, Tuburbitan martyrs, in Africa or from Tuburbelucenaire. Instead of cultivating the religion of Jesus in secret peace (since it was then a novelty) and tenderly raising her children, Crispina defied judges and her sovereign and went to meet the torment that maternal love would have made her avoid.

As for the three others, we learn only that they died for their faith in the second or third century. Which sufficed for the gratitude of the Church to grant them a special cult. Fine!

The Holy CROSS. See Saint HELEN or stay with this heading.

Saint CUNEGONDE, empress, widow and virgin. Empress, widow and virgin! Only in the Church do we see the most heterogeneous things amalgamated. Cunegonde, who since her childhood had a very tender love for Jesus, was nonetheless married to Henry, king of the Romans.[16] (What would the ancient republicans have said to a prophet who announced to them that they would one day have kings, and saints as kings!) But here is how these two august spouses employed the time of their union. Daytime was destined for the active life, and night for contemplative life. Those are fancy words that only express very natural things. Their lack of taste for carnal joys didn't, however, prevent the husband from suspecting the fidelity of Cunegonde.

What was the empress's defense? Women of our century, lend an ear and shudder! Cunegonde marched barefoot on red-hot plow blades without being burnt. Certainly it's right that this barbaric test has been banned. If it took place, what would become of the tiny foot of our elegant women?

From then on, the emperor believed in the honor of his wife, with as much faith as in the gospel. Our modern husbands might not be less incredulous. After her husband's death, Cunegonde abdicated the throne – which, indeed, wasn't her place – and died a nun. Other times, other mores. I forgot to say that Cunegonde fed herself only once every Wednesday and Friday. I also forgot to say that Poland owes its salt mines only to the prayers of this saint. It is true that in her time, natural history was less known than sacred history.

Saint CYRE, see Saint MARANNE.

D

Saint DAFROSE. Saint Damien, her husband, was a martyr. Was he the martyr of his wife? That could be concluded according to the honors the latter obtained in the Church, born enemy of terrestrial virtues. Whatever the case, Dafrose, as a widow, was banished under Julian the Apostate,[1] born enemy of speculative virtues.

Saint DARIA, virgin and martyr, at Rome, and subsequently Saint Chrysanthus, her husband or whatever you like, but a martyr. They say that this saint was a "virgin of Minerva" and that she was buried alive in the "criminal's field" because she left the "flame of Vesta" for Saint Chrysanthus.

Saint DATIVE, Saint DENYSE, Saint LEONCE, Saint VICTORIA, all four martyrs under the Vandals.[2] These four blessed girls were stripped nude in a public place and whipped. These four virgins preferred to show the people all the treasures of modesty rather than to conceal their cult. Only saints are capable of such edifying behavior.

Saint DENYSE, Saint MERCURY, and two other saints named AMMONAIRE, martyrs at Alexandria. Typical martyrs.

Saint DENYSE, virgin of Lampsacus. This holy girl would rather be delivered, at sixteen, to the secular arms of two young men, than offer incense to the chaste Diana.

DEBORA and JAEL, the one a governor of the Israelites, judge and prophetess, the other murderer of Sisera. These are two saints of the Old Testament, as will be noticed by what follows. One was for consultation, the other for execution. Since the Jews did everything in the name of God, who guided their hand, Jael, fortified by grace, went to find the enemy general, "got him extremely drunk," and nailed his head to the ground. It was Debora who gave her permission. The Israelites sang a *"Te Deum"*[3] in gratitude for such a fine event which visibly announced the finger of God.

Saint DENYSE, see Saint DATIVE.

Saint DELPHIRE, wife of Saint Elzear who was count of Arian and baron of Ansouis; nevertheless she was a virgin. The first night of their marriage, between these two married saints left alone and safe from the fracas of tumultuous festivals, there occurred quite a strange scene. The young wife halted her husband's first movement, telling him that the "treasure" he wanted to rob her of wasn't hers; that the celestial spouse had chosen it and reserved it for himself alone. Elzear didn't insist that night. Apparently he knew women, and probably was a good-tempered person...To this point, nothing miraculous; it's a commonplace of all young women. But what will surprise is that the husband didn't advance his conjugal duty any further on the following nights than on the first; for, having only one bed, our spouses, each armed with a little iron chain, administered discipline to one another with all the fervor worthy of a better cause. The legend, which sometimes is reasonable, is careful to warn us that it doesn't offer these two spouses as an example to follow; and assuredly it does well to do so because it would have won few proselytes and would have found few believers.

Saint DODE, see Saint BEUVE.

Saint DODE, wife of Bishop Arnoul. It's edifying to see a holy woman the wife of a bishop.[4]

Saint DOMITILLA, Roman martyr. Domitian exiled her to an island. She was followed there by Nereus and Achilleus, who were, it is claimed, two of her eunuchs and who were saints and martyrs with their mistress. For the edification and tranquility of our readers, we will not discuss this historical point.

Saint DOMNINA. See Saint BERENICE, her daughter.

Saint DOMNINA and Saint THEONILLA, martyrs in the same place and at the same time. It would abuse the patience and sensitivity of our readers – especially our women readers – to follow here the legend, which, sure of pleasing, never fears to bring in the least agreeable details of the torture of its martyrs. Besides, these too-frequent instances have become clichés which might no longer make any impression on our blasé contemporaries.

Saint DONATILLA, see Saint CRISPINA, her companion.

Saint DOROTHY of Alexandria. This virgin and martyr was a philosopher at the same time. She found grace before Maximien d'Aja, or Galere, who was the Attila[5] of the maidens of Alexandria. This prince let her keep her life, but "contented himself with stripping her of her property." (Are others struck, as we are, by the legend's decency of expression?) Having nothing left to lose, Dorothy was banished from her country, around the year 306. They don't say how the lovely Dorothy was able to soften the great persecutor of Christians, especially virgins. As a philosopher perhaps she placed herself bravely above minor scruples, such as the prejudices of her sex. For the rest, this silence, this limitation of the sacred history, has nothing obscure for anyone who understands a hint.

Saint DOROTHY of Cappadocia. Fabrice, governor of Caesarea, was perhaps less hostile to the religion than to the virginity of this saint. It is reported that before being condemned, "Dorothy sent two apples and three roses" to a young lawyer named Theophilus, who had challenged her to send him flowers and fruit from the garden of her divine spouse. This incident can serve to convince us more and more of the "decorum" that the martyrology so closely observes in its recital of deeds which are the least susceptible to decorum. We may well judge whether the betrayed governor inflicted martyrdom on this virgin-spouse, who had displayed for someone other than himself the treasures of the husband-god to whom she was consecrated.

Saint DYMPNA, virgin and martyr, at Ghele in Brabant. We will see by way of history whether the Church is right to define her as a virgin and martyr. Here is the story in two words. To avoid the incestuous embraces of her father, she took refuge in the arms of a priest. Her father pursued her and destroyed her along with her holy guide.

Saint EDELBURG or AUBIERGE, EDELBURGA or EDELBURGIS, abbess of Farmoutier, and Saint ARTONGATHE or ERCONGOTE, nun in the same abbey; and CARCONGATA or CORTUNGODA. Those are some barbaric names! These two nuns were daughters of two kings of England. Apparently they owe their altars only to gratitude. Benefactresses of their convent, they didn't have far to go to become its patrons, and for that we give praise to ecclesiastical discipline.

Saint EDILTRUDE. This is the same as Saint AUDREY or ETHELDREDE or ELIDRU.

Saint EDITH, virgin, nun of Wilton in England. Born, so to speak, in the convent where she lived and where she died at the age of twenty-three, this virgin, thirteen years after her passing, appeared to a holy prelate to order the raising of her body and to let him know in advance that he "would find it without corruption other than the parts which she had used badly." In fact, adds the legend, with the exception of her thumb, with which she was accustomed to make the sign of the cross, all the other parts of her body were "spoiled and rotten." This anecdote scarcely does honor to the convent of Wilton in England.

Saint ELIDRU, see Saint AUDREY.

Saint ELISABETH of Hungary, landgrave of Thuringia and Hesse, widow. The legend would be the finest book of practical morals if all the sainted personages whose lives it describes resembled this beneficent sovereign. How delightful our task would have been, and interesting for our readers, if we had only had saints of this mettle to report!

The Blessed ELISABETH of Malatesta of the order of Saint Claire. She was a headstrong person, this Elisabeth of Malatesta. When she was a widow – and perhaps she hurried to be one – she connived so much on behalf of a certain Féligny that the pope, Nicolas V, put her in the convent; force determined her vocation, and she made a virtue of necessity.

The Blessed ELVIRA of Ville-Seiche. This woman made her house a convent when she became a widow; this requires no miracle, and there was nothing to make her a saint. So Elvira is only blessed.

Saint ELISABETH of Portugal, queen and widow. The most unbelieving philosopher would be edified by the life of this august sovereign, who didn't think herself quit of humanitarian obligations when she had fulfilled those of a devotion sometimes puerile and overscrupulous. This good princess ought to have enlarged the list of martyrs, for she was the wife of a jealous husband.

Saint ELISABETH, mother of Saint John the Baptist. Up to the sixteenth century, this good friend of the Holy Virgin was totally forgotten. Cardinal Baronius made up for this silence. Besides, we didn't have enough saints yet. The more crazies in the world, the more people laugh. The more saints in paradise, the better it will be.

Saint EMILIANA, see her sister, Saint THARSILLA.

Saint EMMA, see Saint AME or AMEE.

Saint EMMELIE, mother of the great Saint Baile and of many other children, all saints. This was a good enough mother of a family, but she'd rather make saints of her children than citizens.

Saint ENNATHA or ENNATHAS, virgin martyr, in Palestine. This saint was burnt alive after having been dragged naked through the crossroads of the city of Scythopolis near the lake of Genazareth. Does the Church, which so pompously displays the names of its martyrs and the disgusting details of their tortures, think thereby to give them great weight? We dare to doubt it, and we fear that phlegmatic people might be horrified at a religion which has produced so many blind fanatics and which creates so many innocent victims.

The Holy THORN. See the passion of our lord Jesus Christ, and read it to the end if you can.

The Holy SPONGE. Same.[1]

Saint ERCONGOTE, see Saint EDELBURG.

Saint ERMELINDA or HERMILENDIS, virgin. Native of Louvain in Brabant, this young saint, "very young," abandoned her father and mother to follow her spouse Jesus. Every evening she went to church barefoot. A little sacristan came out, without complaining, to open the doors for her, and "to chant with this virgin the nighttime office." In vain did two young lords undertake to corrupt the little porter. Faithful to Ermelinda, he was not eager to expose to the teeth of ravishing wolves the delicate lamb whose favorite shepherd he was.

Saint ESPERANCE, see Saint FAITH.

ESTHER, mistress of Ahasuerus king of the Persians, and Old Testament saint. What a good mother is the Church! With what solicitude she watches over the health and salvation of her children. Every condition finds grace in her eyes. With what indulgence she hastens to sanctify even human weaknesses. What king could read the story of Ahasuerus without wishing to meet another Esther...!

Saint ETHELBURGE. The sister of a sainted bishop couldn't avoid being a saint.

Saint ETHELDREDE, see Saint AUDREY.

Saint EUDOCIA, that is, good reputation. The celebration of this sainted allegory falls on the first of March. Young virgins, don't fail on that day to burn a grain of incense on the altar of good reputation.

Saint EUDOXIA, virgin martyr. Like most other virgins and martyrs.

EVE, mother of the human race. This sex is so fragile, and the demon of the flesh so tempting! There was only one man on earth, and Eve doubtless had natural energy even in her earliest youth. What reasons to excuse her! But just because the indulgent Church wants to consecrate a cult to the memory of Eve—women: don't conclude that to merit the same honors you have to treat your husbands as she treated good old Adam.

Saint EUGENIA, virgin and martyr, at Rome. This saint was a virtuous virtuoso, a pretty and spirited Roman lady who was converted by the epistles of Saint Paul—which, however, doesn't speak well of her erudition or her taste for literature. Then, disguised as a man, she withdrew to a monastery, became "abbot and father of the monks" (says the good bishop Avis) and returned to Rome to suffer an unspecified martyrdom.

Saint EULALIA of Barcelona, virgin and martyr, commonly called Saint OUILLA, OLORA, AULAIRE, AULAYE. This was a little energumen who, having gone off her head, went up against Ducian, governor of Barcelona, and made so much noise that this minister of Diocletian[2] had her stretched on the rack. True, there weren't yet any madhouses.

Saint EULALIA, virgin and martyr, from Merida in Spain. She is also called AULAYE or OLAILLE. This was a little girl of twelve who, according to the character of her age, wanted to copycat the martyrs whose history had upset her brain. Little Eulalia went before the judge, spat holily in his face, broke the idols, and trampled the incense and wafer meant for the gods. The judge ought to have let her go with a whipping and returned her to her parents; they say he condemned her to the flames. The grave Saint Prudence assures us that when the little saint had given up her spirit, people saw "fly from her mouth a white bird in the form of a pigeon." (The instructed Christian knows that the Holy Spirit disguises itself as a dove when it deigns to visit mankind.) The same father of the Church adds that when the flames were extinguished, a great quantity of snow fell on the body of the martyred child, which was exposed nude in the place of execution; but the legend does warn us that it was the middle of winter, so this was not as miraculous as the next incident. Before the altar where they placed the relics of Eulalia, there were three trees, which every year are covered with flowers on her feast-day, which falls on the tenth of December.

Saint EUPHEMIA, virgin and martyr from Chalcedonia. They broke her teeth and burned her. That is all we know for sure, and even that is only known because of a scene described by a bishop.

Saint EUPHRASIA. First the wife of Saint Namat, she made herself a nun when her husband left her to marry the archbishopric of Vienna. We probably owe the sanctity of Euphrasia to her spite. Certainly Namat didn't act like a gallant man. All the bishoprics in the world — are they worth the chaste kisses of a holy spouse?

Saints EUPHRASIA, mother and daughter, recluses in Thebaide. The mother was a wealthy widow who ought to have been given a tutor, for she only used her goods to favor the laziness and ignorance of an infinite number of recluses, who lived like wild animals, broke all their links to society, and would have led everyone, if they could, to a state of pure nature. You may judge by only one of their rules: they regarded bathing as a crime and congratulated themselves at maggots in the filth of their baptismal water. The daughter was more excusable than her mother. Not knowing the world, she had the courage to be pleased with these places, for her mother led her from cell to cell as an education. But nature, which never loses its rights, made her suspect from time to time that there existed a sex for which she was born. The Beguines told her that these prickings of the flesh were the work of the demon. She had to believe it and go along with it. Besides, the expectation of one day being a superior and having the right to give discipline engaged her at first to receive this advice with docility, so that the austerity of penance was only the effect of ambition, which dominated her and led her to the grave aged only thirty years – too late for her happiness.

Saint EUPHRASIA. See Saint CLAUDE or the seven octogenarian virgins.

Saint EUPHRASIA, that is, the well-spoken saint. The Athenians would have made her the goddess of speech, the divinity of eloquence. But we have the Holy Spirit, who graced the apostles with the gift of tongues.[3] Was Saint Euphrasia a contemporary of Saint Chrysostom, or golden-mouth? We don't have time to verify this fact.

Saint EUPHROSYNE. At eighteen, this virgin, in whom "charity" had by far outstripped her age, fled the house of her birth, abandoned father and mother to take refuge in a convent. So far the reader finds nothing extraordinary; but it was a convent of a dozen recluses that she preferred to one single carnal husband. Such is the power of vocation. Wicked jokers will add, "or rather, of temperament." The dozen solitaries willingly gave her a man's outfit and had no wish to broadcast this pious secret. Thus Euphrasia spent thirty-eight years among these charitable monks, under the name of Smaragdus, and was careful to reveal nothing to her parents except in her death-message. What was she risking? She had lived.

Saint EUSEBIA, or EUSOYE, or YSOIE, abbess of Humaye. Eusebia, from the age of eleven years, was abbess and had the faults attached to that position. Her mother was obliged to administer correction to her. On this topic we transcribe exactly a note we have found in the holy martyrology. "Our mores and our habits do not permit us to report further circumstances." Our readers can give free rein to their imagination and to their ordinary sagacity, in a matter which is no doubt quite susceptible to both.

Saint EUSTOQUIA or EUSTOCHIA, virgin, daughter of Saint Paul. See her mother.[4]

EUSOYE, see Saint EUSEBIA, it's the same.

Saint EUTROPA, virgin and martyr, sister of Saint Nicaise, bishop of Rheims. The poor girl sought out nothing less than the honors of martyrdom. She was enveloped in the massacre that the Vandals committed at her brother's home. But the Church — which loves, above all, to make crowds — hasn't neglected the memory of this innocent saint who hoped from the barbarians something other than blows of a sword.

Saint EUTROPA or EUTROPIA, widow, in Auvergne. She was a good wife, good mother, wise widow; we don't know how or why the Church was able to make a saint of her.

Saint FABIOLA, see Saint BABIOLA.

Saint FARA, virgin, abbess of Farremoutier in Brie; in Latin, BUGUNDOFARA. When her parents wanted to marry her off, the young Fara fell ill. At first they didn't concern themselves overmuch as to the cause of this setback, but eventually, through information, they learned that the young girl "had consecrated her virginity in the hands" of a certain Saint Columban, who, passing through Meaux, had lodged in the home of our abbess's family and had given to this virgin "a special private benediction." We respect the work of the Church; Fara was abbess during her life and a saint after her death.

Saint FAUSTA. Wife of the emperor Constantine,[1] Fausta was a saint, we aren't too sure why. Perhaps we will know some day. While waiting, let us not forget to put a donation in her box.

Saint FELICITY, mother of seven martyrs. Only religion could offer such scenes. A mother who declares to the judges that her children are Christians and thus deserving death, who leads them herself to the scaffold, and doesn't die without seeing the last of her children die....

Saints FELICITY and PERPETUA, martyrs. Perhaps it's not without foundation that these two saints are accused of having had their minds turned to visions and are charged with "montanism."[2] Indeed it's the only justification one might be able to give of their conduct. We will not enter into details that would be repugnant to the delicate sensibility of our woman readers. But if to be saint and martyr it is necessary to trample on the most inviolable natural sentiments, they have well deserved their place in the holy almanac. To dishonor a family, cause a father to die of sorrow, to see with dry eyes his despair, to abandon a baby boy at the breast and cause the death of another even before he can be born — that is what this martyrized couple did — or rather the fanaticism of which they were the instrument. O virtue! O truth! You have no martyrs comparable to those of superstition.

Saint FELICULA, Roman virgin martyr. Since we are not writing a novel, we will rest content here with just the title.

The Blessed FELICIA de Milon, of the order of Saint Claire. Like most nuns.

The captive woman, apostle of the Iberians, Saint CHRISTIANA, servant. The Church, whose fine politicking could be proverbial, might have shown it to better advantage, in our opinion, when she laid the foundations of her vast edifice. Why did she not confide to women the missions that she distributed to her apostles? A Mary Salome, a Samaritan woman, a Martha, and so many others – or else we are deceived – would have done a better job than a Peter the fisher, a Matthew the clerk, etc. If proof of our assertion is wanted, the saint in question will serve. She alone, through her miraculous babble, converted an entire people.

Saint FLAVIA or FLAVIANA. This is the sister of three saints, who is scarcely known except in Auxerre.

Saint FLORA and Saint MARIA, virgins and martyrs in Spain. "Pagan or profane mythology," as is known, counts among its more amiable divinities a goddess Flora, mother of flowers and lover of Zephyr. The legend, which could be called "sacred or holy mythology," was the rival of paganism and opposed to it a Saint Flora, who was not, however, comparable to the first one. Saint Flora is a disagreeable character who lets her hair be torn out to defend a cult she doesn't understand, and who, along with a certain Maria, braves the authority of the judge and gets her head cut off.

Saint FLORENCE, wife and martyr, in Narbonnaise Gaul. This holy woman became a martyr on seeing martyrs. New anecdote that justifies the force of example.

Saint FLORENCE, virgin and not martyr. This one was sister of two bishops. She must have entered heaven with great pomp.

Saints FAITH, HOPE, CHARITY. Latin: FIDES, SPES, CARITAS. Greek: PISTIS, ELPIS, AGAPE. Sisters, virgins and martyrs, with SOPHIA their mother, a widow. Never have saints' names been as particularized, and never has less been known than of these saints. It is said that only the mother of our martyrs, Sophia, or Wisdom, died "in peace," three days after having seen and provoked the martyrdom of her daughters. This false mother was a good Christian and hardly resembled that modern mother who, hearing the story of Abraham,[3] responded, "God wouldn't have asked that of a mother."

Nota bene. The name of these four saints generates an idea. Perhaps they never existed. Perhaps it's only an allegory, to make us understand that faith, hope and charity are the offspring of wisdom.

Saint FAITH, widow and martyr, at Agen. We will only give the title rather than repeat commonplaces which won't instruct and, worse, won't amuse.

Saint FRANCES, Roman lady, widow, founder of the Collatines.[4] This Frances ought to be the patron of prudes. She was one herself, so much so that she couldn't tolerate the innocent caresses of her father. This meant she had the greatest disposition to be a saint. After having lived some time with her husband, she decided to take a separate bed. We don't know how the spouse took this new lifestyle that his wife prescribed, all the while claiming to be his servant. But he died shortly afterward, and Frances could finally turn herself over to meditation, to her evangelical ecstasies. Luckily Frances didn't leave many imitators; her example didn't catch on.

Saint FRANCES, another Roman lady. The legend would be truly a golden book if it had admitted only saints of Frances's character. This lady once left the divine office of mass to obey her husband. Returning to the church, she found the line where she had stopped in the prayerbook written in letters of gold. I don't know any parable more clever and more moral than that.

Saint FRANCULA, see Saint LINDRU, her sister.

The Blessed FRANCES, nun of Saint Claire. This one only performed miracles after her death. In mid-winter, roses were seen to grow and flower on her tomb. This metamorphosis is a bit renovated from the Greeks.

Saint FREWISSA, English nun; in Latin, FRIDESWIDA. Friend reader, go on to another if you seek the useful and agreeable. This saint will furnish you neither.

G

Saint GALLA, widow, daughter of the consul Symmachus.[1] Let this saint's vocation for religious life be judged by this incident: widowed during the first year of her marriage, and "born with an extraordinary temperament for one so young" (these are the terms of the legend), doctors ordered marriage for her as an indispensable remedy, and "added that there was no other way to avoid growing a beard; anyone else" (adds the legendary) "would have shuddered at the menace of such a humiliation." But Galla resigned herself to this disgrace, which indeed occurred. She cloistered herself and died of a cancer which devoured her breast: sad effect of her thoughtless and reckless decision.

Saint GEMMA. The Bollandists[2] themselves didn't know what to say about her.

The Blessed GENEVIEVE, patron of the Parisians. About the year 429, Germain and Loup, both bishops and both saints, stopped while passing through Nanterre. Germain noticed a little girl of eleven years old, took her aside, has her dine with him, and at dessert makes her swear to die a virgin. Perhaps there already wasn't much time left. This little girl was the Blessed Genevieve. An illness whose type is unknown came over her a few years after having made her vow and her consecration to virginity. She was unconscious for three days. We regard this three-day swoon as one of the main miracles in the life of this saint. However, not everyone interprets these vapors positively. The reader will note that Genevieve lived in Paris at the time.

This circumstance can throw a ray of light on the nature of her indispositions. Germain returned to Paris during this time, and doubtless he vigorously took up the defense of her whom he had placed among the number of his virgins. The bishop having departed, evil tongues began once more their cackle against his protégée. They went so far that the good prelate was obliged to send a deacon assigned to "lambs,"[3] who appeased the malcontents and rescued Genevieve.

The Parisians didn't know the treasure they possessed in her person. Childeric, father of Clovis, whose conditional conversion is known, besieged the capital of the Gauls, and having made himself master of it, wanted to massacre all the inhabitants. To do so he had to close the gates, but they opened in the presence of Genevieve. This second Esther went out of the city walls and offered herself to the desires of the prince in order to disarm him – apparently he looked like Ahasuerus to her – and the Parisians owed their salvation to the pious abandon of their patron.

A miracle more difficult to believe than the one we just reported was the reconstruction of the church of Saint Denis, which Genevieve accomplished with the same ease that God, some thousands of years earlier, built the world, the labor of a breath.

We are committed only to certain and little known facts. As for the others, we will make a scruple of conserving their tradition. We will copy here only a few couplets of a song addressed to a friendly widow, to show our benign readers the point to which one is permitted the license to write on the most respectable things. To refute disbelieving libertines, it suffices to quote them:

IMPIOUS COUPLETS
Addressed to an amiable widow, who had Genevieve as her patron

Run promptly,
Too credulous passersby!
To get the Indulgence
Wasted on fools.
By another Genevieve
Our hearts are captured
Who, better than Eve,
Would get us chased from Paradise.

The patron saint of Paris
Is virgin, so they say.
However, they give her
Marcel, companion gay –
In the same field they meet
Next to all their sheep;
But did they meet this way
Always to pray?

Choose, then, as did she,
A companion in love.
Take her as your model:
You'll be a saint some day.
The almanac of Cythera
Will include your name;
To a widow who pleases,
One has devotion.

To your holy chapel
With zeal men will go;
In its narrow boundaries
A candle we'll make glow.[4]
Of our trembling virgins
Genevieve is the support,

Of our suffering widows
You'll calm the worried heart.

Saint GERTRUDE, virgin, abbess of Nivelle in Brabant. We are no longer surprised at the good luck that the name of Gertrude has created in the world, and we admit that this saint is the worthy patron of women we call "Lady Gertrude." Our saint, at the age when one learns the catechism, refused as husband a handsome and well-made young man. She was still ignorant of the use and value of one, so nothing surprising in this refusal. But when she had reached the age of fourteen, a certain bishop named Saint Amant became her director. This man of God was attached to no diocese; he traveled, recruiting virgins everywhere and building cells for them. He lodged with Gertrude's mother, who was widow of Pepin, prince of Brabant, mayor of the palace under Dagobert, and he placed "the seal of virginity on Gertrude" who, as recompense for her docility, was elected abbess. One of the "great pleasures" of our saint was to give hospitality to wandering priests without shelter. Despite the deprivation of the century the example of Gertrude is still followed.

Saint GLOSSINE, virgin, abbess at Metz, CHLODESINDIS in Latin. Allow us a remarkable preliminary! It is that we have never encountered so many virgins as in this legendary. If it is an effect of grace, we'd have to believe that grace has been withdrawn from us along with the gift of miracles. O our friends and brothers! Have a little religion, a little faith, even if only to meet virgins.

To return to our saint: she had such an aversion to marriage that she resolved to let herself die of hunger rather than to leave the cathedral where she had taken refuge in order to escape the urging of her parents, who wanted to marry her off. And why force people? If they hadn't spoken of marriage to our holy maiden, the taste for it would have arrived anyhow, perhaps all too soon. We would have placed the fine resistance of Glossine in the rank of the most outstanding miracles, but an anecdote which the legend itself brings to our attention halts us abruptly, and this is regrettable. The sacristan of the church provided for all the physical needs of our virgin, and grace for all the spiritual needs. With this help she could have lived for a century and sustained the siege without capitulating. For her reward she became abbess and, what's worse, saint.

Saint GODEBERT, virgin, at Noyon. What to say about her? Her story won't be long and doesn't apply to her alone. She came into the world to live and die in a cloister.

Saint GODELIEVE or GODELEINE, married woman and martyr; in Latin, GODOLIVA. They say that the season for saints and martyrs is past, but there never were as many as today, if what it takes is to not get along with one's husband and wind up the victim of a bad marriage. Such is the story of the sanctity and martyrdom of Godelieve. From another angle, though, there never were fewer saints than at present, if canonization is granted only to docile and patient women – such, in a word, as the Church shows us in Godeline.

Saint GORGONE or GORGONIA, sister of Saint Gregory called the theologian, and of Saint Cesar, daughter of Saint Gregory of Nazianzen and of Saint Nunna. Did the Church intend with this profane name[5] to depict the ferocious virtue of this saint? A smile never lived on her lips. The least hint, the most innocent gesture wounded her chaste ears or her always watchful eyes. She was a dragon in honor. Covered with rags, she thought that the art of pleasing was a work of the demon and therefore tempting. She only let up in the presence of priests. Nothing hidden for them. New Jasons,[6] they had the right to approach the fleece and the apples of this rude Hesperide. Without a miracle that God made expressly for her, Gorgon would have died rather than allow the eye or finger of the most discreet and decrepit doctor to penetrate the dark avenues of the sanctuary of modesty. When a troublesome illness attacked that sacred place, she had the remedy ready and administered it herself. She made herself an ointment with water and her tears (for heaven had given her the gift of tears), the "anti-types" of the body, etc....

N.B. What we are suppressing here, the legend had the courage to write in full. See our grand-uncle Adrien Baillet in the article "Gorgone."

Saint GOULA or GUDULA. Daughter, sister and sister-in-law, cousin and god-daughter to saints, Goula (this name is not very noble)[7] was born in Brabant, in the seventh century, and often mortified her flesh to merit being the spouse of Jesus. We only mention her because of the singularity of her name.

Saint GUIBORAT, recluse virgin and martyr, in Switzerland, and her companion, Saint RACHILDA. Vilorade, or Guiborat, through the power of devotion, was a little bear from childhood on. She wouldn't see any of her relatives – I lie! – the holy chronicle speaks of a brother who was the exception and found grace in the eyes of his sister. She made clothes for him, ironed his underwear, and withdrew with him when Hitton (thus he was named) became a priest. The brother and sister together performed the offices of day and night; in a word, they were so intimately linked that gossip circulated about them so that anyone else than a saint would have been alarmed. She only left this dear brother to live as a recluse with a young girl named Rachilda. Our saint didn't have ordinary tastes! Everything went well in their cell until the arrival of a treacherous widow who wanted to share their lifestyle but who didn't have a religious vocation. She loved sweet apples, and Guiborat gave her only wild ones. The husband of Wendilgarde, this third woman, reappeared (they had believed him dead). In leaving the two recluses, Wendilgarde naively promised to consecrate to Saint Galla the first child she would have. She did have one, but she paid for this pleasure with her life. As for our heroine, she is wrongly placed in the rank of martyrs, for she wasn't killed for maintaining faith but was the victim of her own impatience.

Here's what happened. The Hungarians came to ravage Swabia. People urged her to withdraw to a fortress. She preferred to expose herself to the will of God and the Hussars who stripped her but, finding nothing in her that met their desires, massacred her with blows of an axe. For several years, they say, the walls of her cell seemed to be soaked with her blood. If she had only had as much common sense as blood!

Saint HEDWIG princess of Poland, commonly Saint AVOYE. This saint of the highest birth and at the same time the greatest merit, was married out of obedience and gave her husband, through compliance, six children. She could conciliate all things with a marvelous intelligence. During her pregnancy, and on the days of Advent, Lent, other fast days, Fridays, Saturdays, the eve of feasts and the feasts themselves, and Sundays, Hymen[1] abstained. After doing her duty for society, Hedwig retired into a convent and there applied herself at her leisure to her pious schemes. It is for her that this bad Latin verse was made:

Quot sunt Presbyteri, tot missas optat haberi.[2]

Everyone has his hobbyhorse. That of our saint was to have mass said by every priest she could meet. Happy are those whose mania is only ridiculous; so many others have criminal ones!

Saint HELEN, empress, mother of the great Constantine: Flavia-Julia-Helena. The father of this sainted empress was an innkeeper in a small town. The emperor Constantius Chlorus – but then only a bodyguard – lived in a little hostel, saw the little Helen there, found her sweet, took her away and made her his mistress, and had as son the Great Constantine. The ways of heaven are impenetrable; it uses every means to arrive at its goal. Now on Calvary[3] hill was built an altar to pleasure. As we see, extremities touch one another. The empress Helen, forgetting by what steps she had climbed onto the throne of the Caesars, ungrateful Helen had this temple knocked down. Thus evil was returned for good. They discovered in the debris that the tomb of Jesus had served as foundation for the temple of Venus. This singular rapprochement is doubtless through permission of God rather than an effect of chance. It was thus that Helen found the true cross and the five holy nails, which have multiplied prodigiously ever since. Such a great benefit was worth a sainthood for the benefactress, and the Church continues to exploit the precious mine that Helen quite innocently caused to be opened.

The Blessed HELEN of the order of Saint Claire. One of the miracles of this saint is that since her death, which occurred in the year of salvation 1242, and up to the present, the nails and hair of her body grow to the point that they are cut from time to time. But a miracle no less great, perhaps, is that this saint was mute for much of her life.

The Blessed HELEN of Saint Anthony, same. Here is her story in two words: daughter of Alphonse III, king of Portugal, she founded in Estremadura a convent in order to be its cook. What a fine thing is Christian humility!

Saint HERLINDA and Saint RENELLE, sisters, virgins and abbesses; in Latin, HARELINDIS and RENULA, REINILDIS, RELENDIS, REINILA. Born in the country of Tongres, these two sisters, who never saw the world, passed their life in the cloister. More excusable than many of their sister nuns, they didn't fall into visions or phantasms of an exalted imagination. They assembled around them all the talents and consolatory arts, and by assiduous labor corrected the abuses of their position. We are astonished that such odd dispositions in nuns should have found grace in the eyes of popes, fabricators of saints.

Saint HERONDINE, see Saint REDEMPTA.

Saint HERMELEINDE. She was and kept herself a virgin despite and against everyone.

Saint HILDEGARDE, abbess of Mont Saint-Robert in the diocese of Mayence. This diocese sends us many saints and hams, to satisfy every taste. As for our saint, not knowing how to pass her time in her monastery, she decided to have visions, daughters of boredom and laziness. What's worse, she had the vanity to write them down and make them public, edited and divided into three works under the modest title of "Scivias," that is, "Know the ways," as if she understood the science of the ways of God. Today, such a work would be still read in the antechamber of abbesses, and would occasionally make worldly people laugh at the expense of the sainted author. But in the century of the great Bernard,[4] this book merited the convocation of a council.

Saint HILDEGONDE, virgin, called Brother Joseph. Cross-dressed as a man, the young Hildegonde followed her devout father to Palestine, where he died. A faithless valet, appointed tutor of the orphan, stole all her goods.

When she returned to Cologne, her country, a canon found this girlie-boy pleasing. He took him on and brought him to Rome, no doubt in order to obtain indulgences which he needed for his schemes. Joseph (the name of our disguised saint) is captured by archers, mistaken for a bandit they sought, submits to the ordeal of fire and is recognized innocent. Relatives of the guilty party pursue Joseph and hang him from a tree. Shepherds arrive, take him down and revive him. Joseph rejoins his canon, lodges with a recluse and, to silence evil tongues — which the sojourn of a handsome boy at a girl's house got going — he encloses himself in a convent of monks. He hides his secret as best he can and was not discovered, they say, until after his death. Monks are no longer so discreet.

We hope that the edified reader will be grateful that I didn't profit from this fine opportunity to make the novel much longer.

Saint HILTRUDE, virgin, recluse of Liesse. She was a complete prude, like many other saints. That's her story in two words.

HOLDA, prophetess. This was one of those predictors of the future that Judaea used to furnish to the nations, as Bohemia does today.

Saint HONORINE. This saint is known only by her traditional cult. Probably she was a small piece in the edifice of the Church.

The Blessed HOMBELINE, sister of Saint Bernard. Tecelin, Burgundian gentleman, had seven children; six boys whom Bernard, one of them, made monks after his own example; and a daughter who preferred to remain at home with her widower father rather than to imitate her brothers. She married a young lord and enjoyed all the honest pleasures of society. To this point we see a sensible woman; but soon we will see nothing more than a saint. Hombeline makes a visit to Clairvaux and her brothers whom she ought to have forgotten as they had already forgotten their family. Bernard, the great Bernard, had the door closed against his sister, who was dressed and accompanied as suited her rank. It isn't in the cloister that one learns how to live. Also André, her younger brother, surpassed Bernard and insulted Hombeline in terms that we report here only with regret. He called her "a well-dressed sack of ordure." Hombeline replied politely, "Let my brother despise my body, fine! But let not a servant of God despise my soul. Let him come, let him give orders. He will find me ready to do whatever he orders." With these words that we have cited because of their singularity, Bernard consented to see his sister.

 He wanted to separate her from her husband right away (says the legend), but at first he contented himself with instructing her and prescribing how she was to behave henceforth with the husband until it should please heaven to rid her of him. Weak Humbeline obeyed precisely the orders of her charitable brother, and they don't say whether the husband found it good; or rather, seeing that her brothers had turned his wife's head, he was prudent enough to divorce her after ten years. Humbeline lived seventeen years under the discipline of her brothers and died in their arms.

 We pity the fate of this young woman. We admire in silence the conduct of heaven. But we can't help complaining against that of Saint Bernard, who impudently appointed himself its interpreter.

Saint HOU or HOYIDA, see Saint LINDRU, her sister.

The Blessed HUMILIANE. This saint deserved to be a full saint as martyr of conjugal love. The greatest of all miracles is, without doubt, to have always served with fidelity a spouse who was nothing less than amiable.

Saint HUNEGONDE, nun of Semblières in Vermandois. Hunegonde was from the times of Clovis II, king of France. They claim that love of virginity grew in her with her age. The century of miracles is apparently past, for today it's just the opposite. She made a vow, they say, of continence like that of the Holy Virgin Mary – who, nonetheless, was mother at least once. They urged her to marry a gentleman named Eudaldo. Friend reader, guess what our saint is going to do to avoid the yoke of marriage. You think perhaps that she is going to sneak out of the paternal home. She did even better, for to persist in her resolution to remain a virgin and not marry, she undertook a pilgrimage to Rome, and took as traveling companion the one they had proposed as her spouse. On her return, she entered the monastery at Semblières, near Saint-Quentin. What one would never doubt, if one wanted to take the saints literally, is that Hunegonde took as servant and manager of all her affairs both inside and out, the same Eudaldo whom she had refused as husband. This conduct doubtless deserves altars.

Saint ILLUMINATA, virgin. Saint without reality, ideal virgin, to add to the number.

Saint IRENE, see Saint AGAPE.

Saint IRMINE, virgin and daughter of Dagobert.[1] Irmine left her father to follow God – how edifying!

The Blessed ISABELLE of France, virgin, sister of Saint Louis and founder of the monastery at Longchamp. Here, in two words, is the marvelous story of this blessed princess. Vowed to virginity from the age of thirteen years (today this would be considered a little late), Isabelle refused the emperor's hand, in order to have herself tonsured at twenty, by six Cordeliers, and spent all her life being given, or giving herself, discipline whenever she left the confessional – and she went there every day. Assuredly if this woman had failed to reach heaven and canonization, it would have been a great injustice. Could one believe (except for the item on discipline) that Isabelle had any imitator at the court of France in this century? Such a miracle would be worth all hers.

Saint IRIS-BERGE, virgin and sister of Charlemagne.[2] This daughter of King Pepin asked God to make her ugly so as to not have to marry a king of Portugal. This conduct is not natural. The chronicle of the period doesn't say more about it. But are so many reasons needed in order to be a saint?

Saint JEANNE, wife of the intendant of Herod, Chuza. This was one of those women who followed Jesus Christ and his apostles everywhere. She had been cured of a malady whose name the martyrology omits.

The Blessed JACQUELINE of Septisol. Jacqueline was a widow who wanted to try on the rope of Saint Francis. This patriarch had already fascinated her during one of his sermons. She abandoned her children to turn herself over completely to the raggedy-monk saint who, already having Saint Claire, required some pressing to add Jacqueline. She wasn't ungrateful. It is she who sheltered and took care of Francis and his brother friars; she even gave them socks. Francis, who apparently was delicate, like all spiritual directors, took medicinal foods for his stomach, which he needed during his long and frequent conversations with her. Also he called her "his dear" and died in her arms. Jacqueline, widowed for the second time, passed the rest of her days, they say, in weeping on the tomb of her dear patriarch.

The Blessed JEANNE of France, founder of the Annunciad.³ Such are the salutary effects of ugliness: if one has the problem of displeasing men, one has the advantage of pleasing God. That's nature, and Jeanne de Valois, daughter of Louis XI, king of France, resigned herself and did well.

A deformed figure and hideous face were the gifts she had received from heaven, which had designs on her. When you have Louis XI for your father, and for husband a prince who loves pretty women, there is no other choice to embrace than that of devotion; one has to feel a vocation marked for retreat. Repudiated by her spouse when he became king, Jeanne had herself adopted by the Church and tried to console herself by the monastic scepter for the one she had lost. Her confessor Nicolas Gilbert, who had floated this plan to his august penitent, was named superior of the new monastery she founded, and therefore changed his name to "Gabriel of the Ave-Maria." He became thus the director of ten virgins and in consequence gave them as surname the "ten pleasures of Mary." Our cloistered queen died at forty years of age.

The pious reader will observe that it was at six years old that she conceived the project of the Annunciad. It is true that at that age, they like to play at chapel and to dress up their dolls.

The Blessed JEANNE of the Cross, nun of Saint Claire. Little Jeannette, at fifteen years, despite her parents who wanted to make her an honest housewife, made herself a nun; and, despite her parents, the convent superior kept her, I don't know with what right, but I do know with what motive: it was always one more nun. She spent several years in absolute silence: *res miranda*!⁴ Absolute silence suited badly the function of gatekeeper that she exercised. But her destiny was not to remain at the gate; she soon passed to the cathedra and amply compensated for her long and painful silence, in becoming a professional preacher. Today's Church, to reanimate the faith extinguished in the heart of the faithful, especially men, perhaps ought to try this last resource: that is, to make nuns and other women mount the seat of truth as long as they are pleasantly charming. Mute Jeanne soon recovered the word, in preaching. Prelates, cardinals, even an emperor, Charles V, came to hear her. O prodigy of her eloquence! Even an inquisitor softened listening to her, and spouted tears!

Jeannette, pretty preacher, ought to have contented herself with this role and not had her sermons printed. Everything can be good orally, but on paper you have to be more than a pretty woman in order to be read with interest. Also, cooks and lackeys today don't read, or are annoyed or bored by what used to charm cardinals, princes and inquisitors. But a woman can make a hearer weep and not know how to run a household or abuse the pennies of the cashbox. That is what happened to Jeannette, who was deprived of her place as superior. After this little *monitum*[5] she was reintegrated into her dignities, and her past life didn't prevent her being a saint.

JUDITH,[6] widow. It would do injury to our readers to remind them of the life of this generous Jewish citizen, who destroyed her honor for the salvation of her country..."How odd a thing is the Bible!"

Saint JULIA of Africa, virgin and martyr at Corsica. She was from a good family in Carthage, born in the year 439, time of the ravages of Genseric, king of the Vandals. She was sold as a slave to an idolatrous merchant, who was rather happy with her. We may presume that without her babbling, Julia would have been only a saint. But she wanted to have the honors of a martyr and deserved them in speaking indecently of the religion of her masters. She was hanged.

The Blessed JULIANNE, prioress of Mont-Cornillon or Cornouailles, near Liège. The Beguines who presided over her earliest education inspired in her inclinations that could have been higher. Of all the jobs at the convent, Julianne, whether by taste or otherwise, abased herself with the vilest farmyard tasks. Her virginal and pitiless hand daily made capons and killed hens. Right down to the animals, everything felt the spirit of the cloister that she governed. Nonetheless these occupations didn't take up all her time. Of all books, Saint Bernard's commentary on the Song of Songs was the usual and favorite subject of her chaste meditations. Such was the life that merited her only the honors of beatification or semi-sanctity.

Saint CYR and Saint JULITTA, son and mother, martyrs at Tarsus. Julitta, having been arrested as a Christian, stifled maternal feelings to hear only the voice of prideful fanaticism. Saint Cyr, scarcely thirteen years old, cried as loud as he could, "I am Christian." The reader will believe what he can; but he will no doubt shudder on learning that the barbaric mother saw with a dry eye her son crushed on the judge's steps, instance of the insulting egotism of this woman whom the Church honors.

Saint JULITTA, martyr from Caesarea in Cappadocia. Saint Bazile the great made her panegyric; that says it all. He spared us a task which we would perhaps have had a lot of trouble completing, for her martyrdom resembled all the others, and we don't have the right of repetition that the ancient legend has, without annoying our benevolent readers.

Saint JULITTA of Ancyra. See Saint CLAUDE and the seven octogenarian virgins of Ancyra, companions of the innkeeper Theodotus.

Saints JUSTA and RUFINA, merchants and martyrs in Spain. The martyrdom of these two saints is only a women's quarrel, a haranguers' dispute.

    Justa and Rufina were two pottery sellers at Seville in Spain. Other women, carrying a little statue of Venus, entered their shop and politely negotiated for a vase to sacrifice to their idol, which was certainly as valuable as one for a crucified God. Our two saleswomen in their holy rage insult the pagan women, saying, "We have no vessels for this impious use; go elsewhere and learn that Christians adore God and not the monkeys that look like you." "Who are you calling monkeys that look like us?" respond the idolaters, putting down their statue to place their fists on their hips and breaking every item in the shop. Justa and Rufina didn't lose their heads. Not wanting to come off the worse, they grabbed the poor Venus, broke her arms, legs, etc., mutilated her pitilessly and threw her shamefully into the street sewer. Seeing this, the populace riots, throws itself on the two haranguers, and drags them before the governor Diocletian, who gave them the crown of martyrdom, which they no doubt well deserved. The Church in its rituals hasn't failed to inscribe the names of these two women, so that every social level, even those recognized in the marketplace, may have its patron.

Saint JUSTINE, virgin and martyr, at Nicomedia. To chase away the demon of concupiscence, the virgin Justine employed a means that has lost most of its power today. With a sign of the cross, she liberated herself from the recurrent prickings of the flesh. This same sign couldn't liberate her from martyrdom.

Saint JUSTINE, virgin and martyr, patron of Padua. The memory of this saint is as famous as her history is uncertain. No matter! The Church offers to the activity of our faith other objects equally incomprehensible. At Venice they venerate this virgin so much that her name is imprinted on the coinage of the country. Virginity itself enjoys there, as elsewhere, nearly the same honors.

The Blessed JUTTA, tertiary. This Thuringian did not commit a single mortal sin in her life; but when she was widowed, she sold all her goods in order to consecrate the proceeds to the wars in the Holy Land. Do they place this conduct in the rank of venial sins?

Saint LANDRADE, virgin, abbess of Munster-Bilsen in the region of Liège. We remark by way of preliminary that from Liège come as many saints as almanacs.

Her mind exalted by pious Romans, the young Landrade preferred, one fine day, the society of wild animals to that of her parents and fellow citizens, and spent the rest of her life with them. Someone has said that when one is master of the heart one is also master of the rest. We consider that this proposition would be even truer if it were applied to the brain. Travel chronicles have made as many travelers as the legend has made saints. Today the legend makes only unbelievers or libertines.

The Holy TEAR.[1]

Saint LEA, Roman lady, widow. She is known only by a passage in Saint Jerome; and what is known teaches nothing new to the reader who knows, or ought to know, what a Roman lady must have done to merit being beatified by Saint Jerome.

Saint LEOCADIA or LOCAYE, virgin, martyr or rather confessor, in Spain. Spain is a goldmine for the Church. No country is more suitable to making saints, especially since the establishment of the holy and gentle Inquisition. Locaye didn't die during her martyrdom. She only submitted to a long and painful captivity. Others claim that she was thrown from the high ramparts of the city wall of Toledo, her region. If this deed, friend reader, is as indifferent to you as to us, you won't regret the brevity of this article.

Saint LEOCRITIA, see Saint LUCRETIA. These two names are only one.

Saint LEONCE or LEANCIA, see Saint DATIVE.

LEAH and RACHEL, wives of the patriarch Jacob, Old Testament saints.[2] At the age of seventy-seven, Jacob wanted to try marriage. Laban had two daughters. Leah, the elder, had pustulent eyes. Rachel, the younger, was gracious and charming. The good patriarch fixed his choice on Rachel. He got her only after seven years of service. You have to be in the Old Testament in order to take as wife, at the age of eighty, the younger and more appetizing of two sisters! The nuptials are celebrated. Night comes. Good old Jacob goes to bed. They bring in his wife, and it's only the next morning that he notices they've deceived him and that there is a quid pro quo. Evidently good old Jacob had been informed but had neglected the minor details.

The father-in-law, who could well be the much younger brother of his son-in-law, was no fool. He was afraid that Leah might have to stay with him. Good old Jacob was obliged to spend another seven years there; it was the custom of the country. At the end of this time, which was nonetheless well spent, they gave him his dear Rachel, for whom he paid another seven years of his life. Friend reader, let's pause a moment to calculate:

77 years
7 years for Leah
<u>7 for Rachel</u>
Total 91.

At ninety-one years of age to take on two young women! But at that time the Hercules types were so common that they weren't even considered demi-gods.

Leah was fertile, Rachel was sterile and so jealous that she told her husband: "Give me children or I'll die." "Madame" (responded good old Jacob), "do you think I'm a god?" In bygone centuries people were modest, but we will see even better by their deeds that their habits were not like ours. Rachel, demanding justice, gave her servant to her husband. Leah, having always done her duty, also gave him hers. So that good old Jacob, at a hundred, had what he needed to accommodate everyone. This is apparently the origin of the little "Jacob's rod"[3] that they say performs so many miracles. As to the rest, we spare our female readers details which are much better located in the Bible and which they can seek there. There's nothing like looking into the sources.

Saint LIBRA or LIBERA, see Saint LINDRU her sister.

The Blessed LIDWINE, virgin, in Holland. Her life was a continual illness. Thus our least indulgent readers can and should forgive her practical devotions. When the spirit is enfeebled by the body, it feeds itself on chimeras, and perhaps it needs this food. The cruel maladies of this virgin came only, no doubt, from her reckless vow to die a virgin, so that she could be placed in the rank of martyrs of virginity. She had the modesty to compare herself to the Canaanite woman.[4] For a virgin, she chose her models poorly.

The Blessed LILIOSA, martyr. Just like most martyrs.

Saint LIOBA or LIEBE, virgin, abbess, in Germany; in Latin, LEOBYTHA and TRUTHGEBA. Liebe, in German, means "soul" and "love." This last signification little suits a saint and one who was a recluse all her life. It is true that the sacred chronicle says that from the convent that directed Liebe they secretly sent out from time to time babies that had never entered.

Saint LOCAYE. Same as Leocadia.

The Blessed LUCIE of Catalagirone in Spain. Here is this saint's story. Figs tempt her; she climbs the tree. A storm frightens her; she falls from the fig tree into the arms of Saint Nicolas, who spared her a more dangerous fall; and she gradually gets used to carrying the yoke of bishops. There's nothing really miraculous in all this; but enough to merit gratitude and altars to Saint Nicolas, who marries girls off, and had other plans for Lucie. He made her embrace discipline.

Saint LUCE, virgin and martyr from Syracuse in Sicily. Public prostitution was the ordeal of this blessed martyr. The Church has the praiseworthy custom of having saints portrayed along with the instruments of their ordeal. We would like to know how it manages in the case of Saint Luce.

Saints LINDRU, LUTRUDE, or LINTRUDE; and AMEE, AME, EMME, or YMME; and HOU or HOYIDA; MENEHOU or MUNEHILDE; PUCINE; FRANCULA; LIBRA or LIBERA, sisters and virgins from Champagne; under the direction of the priest Eugene. Just like most virgins.

Saint LUCY, great princess of Scotland. One fine morning, the princess left everything: her castle, her lands, her jewels; she went to Lorraine to become a shepherdess and seamstress. Few women have taken the gospel literally, as she did. What a fine book is the gospel!

Saint LUCRETIA or LEOCRITIA, virgin and martyr. Lucretia was the protégée of an archbishop, who raised her near him after having removed her from her parents. The holy protector was publicly whipped as recompense for this service, and Lucretia obtained the bloody palm of the martyr alongside him.

Saint LUDEGARDE, Belgian nun. The story of this saint isn't especially marvelous. Imagine a young girl with a great desire to marry, who begins to enjoy society, to please herself there and want to please, etc., but who has as mother a devout woman. She was sent to a convent as a pensioner. They say that the only pleasure of demons is to recruit companions in their disgrace; good nuns, who do nearly the same, got hold of the impetuous Ludegarde. She took on their headband and was lost to society and to happiness. What does she need with the incense and candles that are burnt in her chapel? A moment of pleasure is worth an eternity of beatification.

Saint LYDIA, dye merchant. This was a lower-middle class woman of the city of Thyetira, or Tyre,[5] in the province of Lydia in Asia Minor, where Saint Paul and his companions often sat at table. We are sure that the Church owes her altars. In those days the Church was grateful for even the smallest service.

Saint MACRA, virgin and martyr in the diocese of Rheims. As our intention is not to make this work an ephemeral and frivolous tract, we contented ourselves with designating the name and qualities of Saint Macra, without entering into greater detail, which could only be found in the fertility of our imagination.

Saint MACRINA, virgin. Daughter of two saints, sister of three saints, and founder of a colony of virgin saints, Macrina couldn't not be a saint herself. She was so lovely, says the holy almanac, that the most famous artists of her time exhausted their brushes on her without succeeding in representing her. In her youth, Macrina committed herself principally to studying the books of Solomon, that chaste author of the Song of Songs. The young man who sought her for the sacrament having died, the Church says that our virgin took this pretext to embrace religious enclosure. The Church, which considers only the edification of its flocks, was not interested in giving a purely human motive for the vocation of the illustrious Macrina. We want to believe in it, and even to invoke Macrina as a saint, without carping at all the details we are given about her life, details that would become insipid for our readers, whose worldly-wise taste longs for piquant anecdotes, which are lacking here to our pen.

Saint MAHAUT, mother of the emperor Othon.[1] Many people are waiting, in order to burn a candle in her chapel, for something more satisfying in connection with her. A saint with an emperor for a son is suspect to many people.

Saint MAGDALENE de Pazzi, virgin, Carmelite. This saint was born in Florence in the year 1566, to the illustrious Pazzi family. Catherine of Siena was her favorite patron saint, and she bore that name until she entered the Carmelites, when she considered it appropriate to change it for that of Mary Magdalene, as if Catherine weren't as good as Magdalene. The martyrology extensively treats the "humiliating temptations," the "revolts of the flesh" that she had to combat. Probably our saint had what is called "temperament." From the age of ten she was admitted to communion. But it was in vain that she so often took her God into herself, for she could only manage to chase out the demon after a great many years.

Saint MARANNE and Saint CYRE, anchorites[2] of Syria. The incredible austerity of the life they led would be considered a prodigy by those who didn't know the force of habit, the power of example, the desire to distinguish oneself, and a thousand other similar little passions.

Saint MARCELLA, Roman lady, widow. This saint understood reason. Widowed after seven months of marriage from which she had a daughter, she refused the pleas of a very wealthy old man, telling her mother that she needed a husband, not an inheritance. Jerome the saint was more her type in every way. She consulted him often about holy scripture, the literal sense of which they practised together. Marcella linked up with Paula (see her life); they deserved one another. Heaven deigned to prove it: the soldiers of Alaric,[3] sacking Rome, entered our widow's home and "pillaged her treasure." Marcella resigned herself to the Lord's will, who allows second causes to act, and died shortly after.

Saint MARCELLA, mother of Saint Potamiane. The mother is known only through the daughter.

Saint MARCELLINE, virgin, sister of Saint Ambrose.[4] It is this saint to whom Ambrose addressed one of his works, entitled "About Virgins," and it was only an obligation he was paying back; for the legend says, in formal terms, that Ambrose had drawn at Marcelline's spring his love for virginity. Nothing more edifying and more orthodox.

The Blessed HYACINTH of MARESCOTTI, tertiary. At seven years old, this illustrious blessed girl, born at Rome, fell into a pit; it wasn't the one of truth, for this fall determined her vocation for the third order of Saint Francis. At fifteen, she wanted to gather the roses of voluptuousness, but an illness whose type and name are not known made her "chew the bitter herbs" of repentance – following the elegant expression of the reverend father Fulgence Ferot,[5] Franciscan friar. God gave her three gifts in recompense for the two confraternities she founded: the gift of prophecy, that of miracles, and, third, tears. The last is fairly ordinary to the sex of our blessed girl. Since she had a cardinal for her cousin, she obtained the honors of beatification, which was accorded her by Benedict XIV, also a relative. It's good to have them everywhere, especially in the Church.

Saint MARCIANNE, virgin and martyr, in the sixth century. This saint was African. Jesus Christ was her husband; in Mauritania, a rather cold husband. One day she went to the public square of Caesarea and, filled with holy zeal that miscreants call something else, she knocked off the head of a marble Diana. This was a mistake; a virgin ought to respect the goddess of virginity. If she had given this treatment to Venus or to Priapus, nothing would have been more orthodox. Couldn't one attribute this violent action to secret resentment in our saint? Be that as it may, the punishment they forced on her was not that of *lex talionis*,[6] for they turned her over to the good will of the gladiators. The legend adds that she was then "exposed to the teeth of ferocious beasts which devoured her." Wouldn't that be a repetition of the preceding sentence? Are we to take these words literally, or are they just a New Testament type of figure, an emblem of the consequences of her first torture, which perhaps wouldn't be a torture for everybody?

Saint MARGUERITE, virgin and martyr, or Saint GEMMA, the pearl of virgins. Everywhere, the Christian world speaks only of Marguerite. If you reassembled her relics, you'd have enough to compose a dozen saints. They vaunt the marvels performed on sterile women after they have worn the sashes sanctified by contact with the relics...and nevertheless it is not verified that Marguerite ever existed. It's too bad that this pearl of virgins should be only a pious lie, a cold allegory of what perhaps never existed. We could, after the example of our predecessors, enter here into agreeable but fictional details. We would rather be less piquant than lack verity. In a profane history one can have fun without scruple, and this liberty is frequently used; but our task imposes duties too sacred for us to be tempted to find adventitious ornaments for it.

The Blessed MARGUERITE, princess of Hungary. Born in 1243 of Bela IV, king of Hungary, they vowed her to the cloister to thank God for having delivered her ungracious, arid country from a barbarian raid. Thus the virginity of Marguerite depended on the outcome of war. The better to fulfill her parents' vow, they put her behind the grill at the age of three years. Apparently they were quite sure of her vocation. She passed twenty-five years in whipping herself and singing Latin psalms; then heaven did her the grace of withdrawing her from the world, where she had felt only the thorns, though born into a rank where one normally knows only roses.

The Blessed MARGUERITE of Cortona. About the year 1249, Marguerite flourished at Cortona: for ten years she worked as a well-known prostitute. The violent death of one of her lovers, whom she had made a father, deprived her of good sense and disposed her to piety. Her heart, empty of love, filled itself with grace. Chased from her region as a madwoman, she took refuge with the Franciscans who, after a trial period of three years, judged her worthy of the blessed rope belt of their founder. She died consumed with the fire of charity. Her son was also a Franciscan and tried, as a preacher, to guide back to the fold the flocks that his mother had once misled to the boudoir.

Saint MARGUERITE, queen of Scotland.[7] In favor of her good qualities, we will pare away those that win her the title of saint. A woman is doubly recommendable when caring for the salvation of her soul, and heaven's glory doesn't make her neglect those of her family and of society. We won't say more about Marguerite; we will observe only that she is one of the saints of whom the legend has spoken most reasonably.

The Blessed MARGUERITE of Foligny, tertiary nun. The masterpiece of this virgin was to return the use of his limbs to a young adolescent. This didn't appear miraculous enough for the Roman prelates to beatify her. Only pious custom established her cult.

The Blessed MARGUERITE of Sulmona, nun of Saint Claire. This saint was from the region of the gallant Ovid,[8] but she had only that in common with the lover of Corinna and Julia. Marguerite was sad and unpleasant; God had given her the gift of tears, which, in winter, falling on her hands, froze there and formed a multitude of pearls – so, agreeably, say the legendary and her predecessor, who apparently had nothing better to say.

MARY, virgin, wife of a carpenter, mistress of the Holy Spirit and mother of a God.

O altitudo!

It has to be acknowledged that the universe was lucky. The mending and redemption of the human race, the salvation of the world, the fulfillment of prophecies, the literal sense and the figures of the Old Testament and miracles of the New, the diaspora of the Jews, conversion of gentiles, destruction of idolatry, etc. etc. etc. – what did all this depend on? A thread, a hair. The destiny of the earth depended on a "Yes" or a "No." If the Virgin had not had such an easy virtue, if she had answered simply "No" to the fine promises and insinuating propositions of the Mercury-messenger of the Holy Spirit, that would have been it. What would have become of us? Alas! We wouldn't have had any Church, no popes, no cardinals, no priests, no masses, no councils, no indulgences, no inquisitions, no crusades, no Saint Bartholomew's Day Massacre,[9] no Carmelites, no little nuns. Mary would have been merely the wife of a carpenter and the mother of a little helper woodworker; the world would have continued to be damned for adoring the mother and little brother of the Graces.

MARY, sister of Moses. Good, she was the sister of Moses.

Saint MARY, said to be from Bethany, and Saint MARTHA. These two sisters — of whom one was probably blonde and the other brunette — one active, demanding, sparkling, the other indolent and difficult to impress or move emotionally; one born for the active life, the other for the contemplative life — were both good friends of J.C. and often rivals. Jesus, who, as every good Christian knows, had a head of hair like the blond Phebus,[10] seems to have leaned a bit more in the direction of the blonde Mary of Bethany than of the dark Martha. The first, continually seated at the feet of her gentle savior, contemplated him at leisure, gathered up his every sigh, and thus proved her love. The other came and went through the house from cellar to attic, prepared meals, ran to the market, and would have been preferred by a gourmand. But Jesus wasn't one. So Martha had only second place in the Christ's heart. No doubt the sisters deserve one in the legend and in the Church's cult.

Saint MARY, called Mary of Cleophas, sister of the Holy Virgin. The finest action of her life was doubtless being born sister of the Virgin. It's well known that in this world, to make the fortune of a whole family, it's often necessary only to have a young and pretty relative who has found grace with the lord and master of the place.

Saint MARY, Egyptian, great sinner and great penitent, patron of courtesans. *Lassata, non satiata viris.*[11] Although it is profane, we would advise young preachers to choose for the sermon or panegyric on this saint, this energetic text of such fortunate application. For those of us who are only historians, we will simply and without exordium begin the story about the life of our Egyptian.

    At twelve, Mary abandoned her father and mother to go to Alexandria where for seventeen years she devoted herself without restraint to all the needs of a "temperament" such as the demon gives to women whom he wishes one day to associate with; or, philosophically speaking, such as the climate produces. We have used the word "temperament" not without reason. Mary, debauched as she was, had a sort of delicacy which proves that, in living this way, she was giving in less to the inclinations of her heart than to the needs of the body. Alas! It is only too common to encounter, in the crossroads of our capitals, dangerous sirens[12] who are more interested in our wallet than in pleasure. Mary, on the contrary, demanded (as the legend says so well) "no other recompense for sin than the sin itself." All other passions were subordinated in her to that of jouissance.

A ship was leaving for Jerusalem. Mary conceives the project of extending the cult of love, her only God, into the country of the God of Christians, and to make the tomb of Jesus serve as Cupid's altar. Mary was poor, but, like the Greek philosopher who carried everything with him (*omnium mecum porto*: I carry everything with me), Mary isn't unable to pay the price of passage. Her favors serve as money to pay off her creditors. We are forced to recognize a type of philosophy in this proceeding. Profane love produced in her what divine love would one day; it detached her from things of the world, rendering her independent and superior to everything. Her sojourn in the vessel responded perfectly to her desires; she made of it a temple to Voluptuousness and earned for Love as many worshipers as she found passengers.

Arrived in Jerusalem, a holy city more corrupt than Alexandria, Mary the sinner hardly thought she'd changed countries and therefore didn't change conduct. For a long time she performed for her divinity all the rituals that pilgrims did for theirs. But she enjoyed her rest, and it was time. Her sect was numerous, and she began to elevate altar against altar. Excess kills beauty. The sinner Mary, at thirty years, had already lived sixty; and after sixty years of pleasure one is no longer suitable for giving it or even receiving it. The loss of her used-up charms, degraded prematurely, worked her conversion.

But from Charybdis she fell into Scylla.[13] The legend, which sometimes takes on the personality of its heroes, says that Mary spent seventeen years fighting in herself the unchristian memories of her past life. Deep in the desert where she withdrew from public view, particularly of men, among whom she could only play henceforth a role hurtful to her self-respect, she entertained only the solitary echoes of dissolute songs she had learned in happier times. A pitiless ardor devoured her. It was only at fifty-one years that she found herself delivered from the tyranny of the flesh.[14] Then she lived like a wild beast. She wandered in the woods without clothing and fled the sight of any traveler; even hermits hardly dared approach her.

One among them, named Zosimus, very old, pursued her as rapidly as his years permitted. At the sight of him, penitent Mary hid herself in the underbrush, crying, "Zosimus, don't come near; I am a woman." She asked for his cloak, if he persisted in wanting to approach. Alas, poor Mary had nothing left to show. We take these details from Zosimus himself, who had them from the mouth of Mary sinner and penitent; who, before dying and faithful to her character to the last moment, still wanted to give the "kiss of peace to the old anchorite."

The Blessed MARY d'Oignies, recluse in the Low Countries. In the year 1177 was born at Nivelle in Brabant a certain Mary of Willenbroek, who made her husband consent to live together as brother and sister, who wept constantly and fell into ecstasy at the sight of a crucifix. They made her a saint; they couldn't do anything else with her.

Saint MARY MAGDALENE, governess of Jesus and, occasionally, sinner and penitent. There is some confusion in the story of this saint. Some claim that Mary Magdalene, cured by Jesus Christ of the seven carnal demons that tormented her, is not the same as another woman who also professed seven diabolical sins. Others (and we adopt this latter sentiment as the more natural) combine the first woman with this one to make only one. Thus we think that the woman with seven demons touched by Jesus is the same as the courtesan named "Myrophora," who came to find him as he sat at table, who slept at the feet of her gentle savior, placed herself behind him, poured on his head and chest tears of love and perfumes, and offered him tender kisses. We know that to the reproaches made to Jesus, he responded only, "I say to you that many of her sins are forgiven because she loves me or because she has loved much."

The successors of Jesus Christ have entered rather well into the spirit of their master.

However, Saint Modest claims that this woman died a virgin. We guess to the contrary that he "did not place enough difference between a possessed woman and a sinner." This woman thus became one of those who followed Jesus everywhere. It was she whom this good master, when he was brought to trial, recommended so tenderly to his cousin John the Baptist. It was before her that Jesus revealed himself after his resurrection and he whom she wanted to embrace — which, this time, she didn't succeed in doing. It was she who went ahead, etc. etc. We know nothing positive about the rest of her life, but what we have just reported doubtless suffices to have made her a saint of the first order. It could be done with less trouble. Her body, headless, is in the choir of the canons of Saint-Savior, at Rome.

Saint MARY Penitent, niece of Saint Abraham. The father of this saint died too soon for his daughter, who lost him at seven years old. Mary had as an uncle a certain anchorite named Abraham. He took his niece and, above all, her goods, which he distributed to the pious do-nothings of the desert, destining his brother's daughter to spend her days in a narrow cell deep in solitude. Only a little window was made to serve as communication between uncle and niece.

The more the young recluse grew, the more she made her uncle remember to pray God for her; she needed that more than ever in order to chase out the demon of the flesh. She attained, as best she could, her twentieth year. The scene is going to change. Another hermit, younger than the uncle, little by little got used to coming to see the niece. At first it was to instruct himself; later, to instruct her. "He did so well" (says the respectable legend) "that young Mary opened her little window to the hypocrite." The cage once opened, the bird didn't stay in it long.

Mary took flight to the nearest city; she sheltered in a hostelry the better to make up for the long abstinence that good old Abraham had made her too rigorously observe. The night his game-bird departed, the old fledgling-taker, who was a visionary, thought he saw in a dream a dove devoured by a dragon. He awakens with a start, runs to his niece's cell, finds it open and deserted. He mourns and appreciates, a bit late, that grace, even efficacious, is feeble when in the heart of a twenty-year-old it has nature as rival.

He has inquiries made and discovers Mary's haven only after two years. This was doubtless by permission of God, who, more indulgent than his representatives, wanted to leave time for Abraham's niece to test out in her own experience the meaninglessness of worldly pleasures.

Good old Abraham, mounted on a sedate ass, goes straight to his niece's lodging. He disguises himself as an old soldier, belts on a sword and covers his time-blanched head with a large felt hat. He doesn't forget to take money.

N.B. The reader will perhaps accuse us of being in contradiction on the subject of this money. First, we are here as elsewhere only the faithful copyist of the legend, which can't be deceived or deceive us. In second place, in furnishing himself, good old Abraham no doubt had recourse to some old friend to get this money. Let the reader take it once and for all as said: the legend is always right, and it can't be judged as one judges a profane novel. Once at the inn where Mary practised "catinism,"[15] Abraham pretended to be a suitor and asked if, for payment, they couldn't have some fun. The innkeeper couldn't help laughing at this aged Adonis;[16] then he called for Mary. The old man, who recognized her, ordered a good supper "& while waiting" (the legend narrates) "diverted himself with her, but managing in such a way that she couldn't recognize him under his big hat." They made merry. At dessert, Mary, who probably was in a hurry, or who was awaiting more modern company, pulled Abraham into her bedroom. Seated at the end of the bed, Abraham allowed himself to be undressed while caressing the beauty whose active hand, endowed with marvelous tact, recognized better than her eyes that she was approaching her uncle. "See, my dear girl" (said Abraham then to his niece), "see now if you recognize me." The reader foresees the ending. Abraham made his niece sit on his steed and brought her back to her cell. Thus ends this pious novel composed, no doubt, for the edification of prudes and the conversion of loose women.

One circumstance that astonishes us, and will astonish our readers, is that the Roman martyrology has totally forgotten this saint. Only the Greeks honor her memory. The educated reader will recall that Athens was much looser than Rome, even modern Rome.

Saint MARY, servant and martyr. This servant saint who as a Christian thought she could lack respect for her masters, was whipped and delivered to the desires of a soldier who, in a moment when even Argus[17] would drowse off, let his prisoner escape. Mary went off to die of hunger and regret among the rocks. The Church, which needs its small as well as its great, seized this occasion to give a patron saint to servants – but in doing so it didn't consult the interest of masters.

Saint MARIA, Spanish virgin, see her companion Saint FLORA.

Saint MARINA, virgin and cross-dressed solitary. Profane ones, impious scolders, disbelieving intellectuals, if you read us, keep yourselves from laughing at the title alone; at least wait until you've read the story of this saint to the end, and don't expect to find here material to interpret. And you, little women, mistresses of vapors, we don't propose here an example to imitate; it would be above your strength; besides, you would never pardon it. But only read, and may grace do the rest of what we will have begun in you!

Marina was called Mary in the world. Those who read history, and especially sacred history, know how many roles this name has played there, and how fortunate it is. Mary was born in Bithynia in the eighth century; she did well to be born then, for later her sanctity wouldn't have had an easy time of it.

Her father, Eugene, withdrew to a monastery to accomplish his salvation, and abandoned his daughter in society to accomplish hers there, if she could. Some time after this separation which the Church approved, but which nature disavowed, the latter won out. It gave remorse to father Eugene, who confided in his superior: "I can't help being worried about my child," he said. This term "my child," which applies to both sexes, fooled the interlocutors. The abbot replied that Eugene could bring the child to him, believing that the father was speaking of a son. Little Mary was therefore brought by Eugene, who cut her hair, gave her a friar's habit, urged her to secrecy and baptized her Marino. Let us admire here the profound decrees of Providence. The salvation of Marina depended on a quid pro quo: neither the first nor the last example of it.

Marina's charms grew from day to day under her robe, and temptations became more frequent in proportion. Her father died, leaving her when she was seventeen. The youngest of the solitaries, harnessed to a little cart, went to get groceries at a market three leagues away. Whether through scruples or false shame or fear of new temptations, Marina avoided sharing this chore with the other friars. They complained to the abbot, and Marina was forced to go there like the others.

In the hostelry where the friars stayed over (for you must know, kind readers, that our robed saints sometimes went to bed), the daughter of the house had listened to a soldier so closely that she carried in her loins the fruit of her intimate conversation with him. The father and mother mistreated the unfortunate girl who, to conceal her lover, placed the blame on the young Marino, who must have had a seductive little face.

The abbot was informed; Marino preferred to confess a fault that he had not committed, rather than confess his sex. Pitilessly "he was punished with all the rigor of discipline" and chased out of the convent, all of which was done without anyone being able to discover his sex. This is, no doubt, a miracle of our saint.

Marina didn't get discouraged; for three years she sat by the door of the monastery and spent the nights lying under the porch. A perseverance so supernatural can have one of the two following causes, and the reader can choose: either it was grace, or a secret inclination which produces at least that many prodigies in the heart of a maiden eighteen years old.

The abbot was touched and let her re-enter, but for penitence they imposed on her the vilest tasks in the convent. Poor Marina swept, brought water to all the friars, cleaned their sandals and stockings, served them night and day — in a word, did all they commanded. Marina succumbed to such rude and frequent exercises. Soon after her passing, the father prior ordered that they wash the body of the defunct boy. Imagine a whole community of robed young men who are suddenly struck with the sight of a female body! The father prior showed not surprise but the keenest sorrow; he tore out his remaining hair and knocked his head against the earth. Finally, he played his role perfectly. He rehabilitated the memory of his dear Marina, who became a saint thereafter and who had certainly earned it.

Saint MARTHA, virgin and martyr in Spain. This Spanish woman was beautiful, like a romance heroine. But she had a mania. When a profane hand wanted to slip a furtive finger under her wimple, she became furious and said: Don't touch that; my two tits are no longer mine; I have given them to my good Jesus.

Saint MARTINE or TATIANNE, virgin, martyr. Like most martyrs.

Saint MARTHA, see Saint MARY of Bethany.

The Blessed MATHIA, of the order of Saint Claire. Like most nuns.

The Blessed MATHILDA or Saint MAHAUT, queen of Germany, mother of the emperor Othon. Wife of Henry nicknamed the birdtaker. While her husband exhausted the state with ruinous wars and made millions of men die, Mathilda extinguished millions of generative acts by instituting at great cost several convents, among which two enclosed 3000 men and 3000 women each. You'd only need two or three similar reigns to destroy the human race! What astonishes us is that only the queen merited the honors of canonization.

Saint MATRONA, servant and martyr. She was servant to a Jewish woman; her mistress had her beaten to death because she was Christian. Others say that this would have happened otherwise had the mistress's husband been at home, for Matrona served her mistress at table, but she was serviced by the master in bed.

Saint MAURA, virgin, at Troyes. The young Maura converted her father, and (as the legend of course says) it was a new spectacle for the bishop to see a grown, bearded man conducted to the foot of the altar by a little girl. After her father's death, Maura passed all her time in churches. It was she who, as the holy calendar reports, filled the oil-lamp of the cathedral priests. It was she who dressed them, ironed their linens, spun their cloth. Saint Prudentius the bishop wore an alb spun, woven and bleached by Maura's own hands. You might think that this gift, every time he used it during a mass, gave him more than one type of distraction during his offices. All these little services were not forgotten. A good deed is never lost. Maura was sainted.

After her crossing over, they washed her body; the water used for this pious duty was converted into milk, "an overwhelming sign that God gave of the virginal purity of his servant." A young man drank some of it and was cured of an illness which the legend, for our edification, calls "a burning fever." A young woman with a birthmark on her cheek, which displeased her husband, washed herself with the milky water and the spot disappeared. If her husband had had a similar spot on his forehead,[18] we'd be curious to learn whether he could have cured himself so easily. For more than two leagues around, the odor of sanctity could be smelt, even by monks. Everything denotes a saint if ever there were one.

Saint MAURA, see Saint BRITTA, her twin sister.

Saint MEURIS, Saint THEA, martyrs in Palestine; Saint MAURA and her husband Timothy, martyrs in Thebaid. Saints Meuris and Thea are like other virgins. Not so Saint Maura, and we don't know if there is great merit in her martyrdom. She was married for only three weeks when they cut out her husband's eyes and ears. Maura interceded for him, also seeking to stir up his faith by the tenderest and most persuasive words that a newlywed can say to her new spouse. Nonetheless they both wound up nailed to a cross opposite each other, despite the silver that the weak Maura had received from the judge to betray her husband's faith.

Saint MAXENTIA or MAIXENTIA or MESSENA, virgin and martyr in Beauvoisis. There is a city which bears the name of this saint (Pont-Sainte-Maixence). She was martyred; she is said to be a virgin; her cult is established in more than one kingdom; her chapel is never without tapers, and still we don't know when she was born.

Saint MAXIME. Lover of the Blessed Germain, bishop of Auxerre. It was at Ravenna at the court of Emperor Valentinian III that she first saw the prelate and promised herself to love him all her life; in fact the faithful Maxime almost never left him, and at his death she wanted to follow his relics on foot when they were translated into the grottoes of Auxerre. She died of fatigue en route; four other sisters, her rivals, were also in the group, but Maxime had first place in the heart of Bishop Germain. Her rare constancy merited the honors of apotheosis. She was buried near the tomb of her beloved. They consecrated an epitaph to her of which here is the beginning: "Here lies Madame Saint Maxime, one of the virgins who accompanied Saint Germain from Ravenna to this monastery."

Saint MAXIME, martyr under the Vandals. Slave of a Vandal, she was married to another slave by her master, who was good. On the wedding night the new husband wanted to treat Maxime as his wife, but the legend claims that Maxime stopped her carnal husband in mid-flight and forbade him to touch any further the spouse of a god. They say that the husband was kindly enough to respect a defense which was perhaps only an adroit encouragement. For the rest, their subsequent conduct was ridiculous, but was it worth the expense of canonization? They ran away from their master's house; he had them pursued and punished as a Vandal knew how to do. They succumbed to this just punishment, which they had further provoked by their religious fanaticism.

Saint MENEHOU or MENEHILDE. See her sister, Saint LINDRU.

Saint MELANIE the elder; Saint MELANIE the younger; ALBINA, Roman lady. The door of heaven is only partially open to Melanie the elder, to punish her for having allowed herself to be taken in by the errors of Origen,[19] and for having chosen the priest Rufinus as her director. Widowed at twenty-two years, only a son remained of all her children. This saint being subject to miscarriages as the legend tells us, she rid herself of the care of raising her only son by going to Egypt, "accompanied by Rufinus," to assist the servants of God there. She went around to all the retreats and distributed her goods among the solitaries. During this edifying maternal career, her son, Publicolus, married a girl named Albina, a saint, and from this marriage was born the young Melanie who, although a saint, didn't run after saints as her grandmother did.

Saint MERCURY, see Saint DENYSE of Alexandria.

The Blessed MICHELINE, tertiary. Widowed at twenty, she consecrated herself to the poor and begged for them; this merited altars. Fanaticism sometimes has good moments and fine aspects.

Saint MONEGONDE, recluse at Tours. Born in Chartres, Monegonde married and bore two daughters whom heaven took back from her in order to make her the mother of a family much more numerous and more holy. The legend means the nuns whom she assembled, after having abandoned her husband who, without children, more than ever needed the company of his wife. Humanly speaking, Monegonde appears to us to have failed her most sacred duties. But when heaven speaks, must one listen instead to the voice of nature? We think so; the Church doubtless thinks not, for it adopted Monegonde as a saint.

Saint MONICA, widow, mother of Saint Augustine.[20] Every good Christian knows this saint, at least by reputation; but what we believe we ought to repeat in order to show the efficacy of grace is that the good Saint Monica liked the fruit of the vine. Even for saints, we must pay tribute, albeit a light one, to the fragility of our imperfect nature.

N·O

The Holy NAPKIN. This isn't a saint but a towel used to wipe the forehead of Jesus, when they took him to the place of execution carrying the instrument of his torture. It is the city of Dijon that possesses this sacred jewel. The folds of this Napkin are still there, as are the spots of fresh blood.

Saint NATALIE. Here is what the legend says; it's a curious passage: "Natalie lent her services to the executioners, to facilitate the martyrdom of her husband, Saint Adrien."

Saint NATALIE SABIGOTHON. Like most martyrs.

Saint NICARETTE, virgin of Constantinople, named, by a nasty transposition,[1] Saint NICERATE. The word Nicarette means "victorious" or "victory of virtue." Our saint is famous through the remedy she administered herself to her bishop, the Blessed Chrysostom, afflicted with something the legend names a stomach ache. It's just a question of understanding; everything is according to the rules.

Saint NICOLE. This saint, not feeling the courage or strength to be completely honest and beautiful, prayed heaven to make her ugly. Her prayer was satisfied; her sacrifice deserved an altar. But someone who could be beautiful and wise at the same time would deserve at least a temple.

Saint NUNNA, mother of Gregory Naz.[2] The mother of a Church father necessarily has to be canonized. However, her name is better than her sanctity.

Saints NUNILLON and ALODIE, sisters, virgins, martyrs in Spain. Two more virgin martyrs; but you don't have to be a saint for that.

Our Lady of the Angels of Portiuncula. In the middle of a January night, the demon of the flesh tempted the good Francis of Assisi. The saint undresses, goes out into the forest and rolls in thorns. He had barely done this two or three times when the thorns changed into red and white roses. He gathered six and brought them to the pope, who without this miraculous metamorphosis would have continued to refuse the indulgence that Francis had been requesting for ten years for his Lady of the Angels, who had appeared to him at Portiuncula, and for miracles which the pope didn't believe. Perhaps it's necessary to believe both or to make fun of both; whatever may be, this is the fact. We see in this story that our legendary-makers have sometimes read Ovid.

Saint NYMPHA, virgin, in Sicily. Saint Nympha! These two words must be astonished[3] to find themselves together. However, the little we know of this saint will justify this strange naming. Nympha was from Palermo, a Sicilian city. Barbarians chased out her bishop, Saint Mamilian. Nympha was his assiduous companion in flight and his consolation in exile. The little village of Soanne served as asylum to their close communication, and there one sees the shared tomb of Bishop Mamilian and Saint Nympha, death having been unable to separate two hearts whom misfortune had reunited.

Saint ODILLE or OTHILIA, virgin, abbess of Humbvenburg or Hombourgen in Alsace. Odille can be placed in the rank of unfortunate children whose barbaric families sacrificed them to ambition. Born blind, she was made by her father to re-enter the nothingness from which he had taken her. To save her from a violent death, they buried her in a convent – not the last of her troubles. For her vision being restored, the first objects that presented themselves to her eyes were shrewish nuns, devout harpies[4] who stupidly martyrized her and made her buy dear the halo that they discerned after her death.

Nota bene. Twenty years after the death of Odille's nurse, the left breast that had nursed her was found to be fresh and ruddy. That's what it is to have a saint as nursling! But this miracle isn't even as important as the one that saved her honor. A rock split open to rescue our saint from the cavalry men sent to pursue her. If maidenhoods have become so rare, the fault for that is God's, for he apparently doesn't attach as much importance to virginity today as in the time of Saint Odille.

Saint OLAILLE, see Saint EULALIA of Merida.

Saint OLORA, see Saint EULALIA of Barcelona.

Saint OLYMPIAD, widow. Widowed very young and scarcely having had time to consummate her marriage, Olympiad wed the Church in a second marriage and passed the rest of her life in the society of six or eight bishops, at the head of whom we have to place Saint Chrysostom,[5] for whom Olympiad performed quite special acts of kindness. The Emperor thought he ought to relieve her of the administration of her great wealth, "wanting to prevent" (says the wise legend) "suggestions of the clerics who directed her." She never wanted to recognize any other pastor than Saint Chrysostom, who ate at her house and whom she provided with everything.

Saint OPPORTUNE, abbess of Montreuil near Almeseschc in the diocese of Seyez. All saints resemble one another, especially those who did nothing but perform the little routine of the convent where they vegetated. Here we will make a remark to serve in all such cases. It's that there are many more sainted abbesses than nuns, although there are many more nuns than abbesses. The reason? It's this: it's ordinarily only to court the existing superior that the previous ones are canonized. Saint Opportune, moreover, was the sister of a bishop who was himself a saint. What entitlement to be one herself! It was a family disease.

Saint OTHILIA, see Saint ODILLE.

Saint OSTRU or AUSTRUDE, virgin, abbess, at Laon; Latin, ANSTRUDIS. Where interesting facts are absent, we are silent. Silence is better than boredom.

Saint OUILLA, see Saint EULALIA of Barcelona.

P

The Venerable Mother Mary of the PASSION, Capucine. Here is a near-saint of recent date (1673) and born in Paris; it's rare to have a saint both modern and Parisian. But she was from the suburb of Saint-Marcel and not from the rue Saint-Honoré.[1] The saintly scandalous chronicle does admit, it's true, in one spot, that when entering the Cordeliers she removed from her parents' house a few valuable jewels, to support a poor scholar toward whom she had kind feelings and on account of whom, at the age of fifteen, she had refused the cold hand of a grave parliamentarian. Since she couldn't do more for young scholars, she went on to the Capucines, chose kitchen work, composed the annals of her order, and lived on the leftovers of the sisters. She died in 1673. Her annals are her spiritual testament, composed in the Capucines' kitchen; they remain in manuscript, like the story of her life, composed by the Perfect Archangel,[2] unworthy Capucin. What a shame to leave such treasures concealed!

Saint PASCHASIA, virgin. Apostle of the Burgundians, Saint Benignus kept Paschasia under his rod for a long time. This virgin territory didn't waste the seed confided to it and bore fruits that still today cause the mouths of Burgundian maidens to water.

Saint PAULA, Roman lady, widow. The Scipios, Gracchi, and Paul-Emiliuses would have been much astonished if anyone had predicted that their family would generate a saint. Originating from these heroes, Paula was born in Rome in 347. Caring for five children, she lost her husband at the age of thirty-two years, and consecrated her widowhood to J.C. Consequently, to please her spouse, she ruined her children and borrowed, without paying back, to give alms to the soothsayers of the new Rome. They say that "she never ate with any man, however holy he might be, not even with bishops." This expression, "not even," made us smile.

During a council held in the metropolis of the Christian world, she attached herself to Paulinus, prelate of Antioch. Was it because of the conformity of his name to hers? We don't believe so, for at the same time she lodged at her house Saint Epiphanius, bishop of Salamine in Cyprus, and also Saint Jerome. The acquaintance of these prelates (acquaintance which doubtless was as completely honorable as it can be between a widow and bishops) so inflamed her "charity" that she could hardly let them leave without her; and certainly she would not have consented to this sacrifice had not Jerome, who stayed on with her, enabled her to tolerate a sojourn of two and a half years in Rome.

At the end of this time, divine love happily triumphed in her heart over natural love. Accompanied only by her daughter, who was a saint like her, she went to Cyprus, where Saint Epiphanius kept her for ten days, "not to refresh her" (says her biographer naively, though he could have dispensed with saying so), "as he had hoped to do, but to inspire her more and more with charitable deeds, which it was her habit to perform everywhere she stopped on the way" (says this same author, our grand-uncle A. Baillet). "She traveled on an ass; she who formerly had been carried by eunuchs." Was it up to the legend to make a merit for her out of this change of mount?

Arrived in Bethlehem, her first concern was to build a monastery for Jerome and his followers, and a second one for herself, her daughter and the virgins who had followed them. We are annoyed to have to report that, among the rules given by Saint Paula to her nuns, she forbade them cleanness of body; she said "it was an emblem of the soul's filth." This rule only suited the Franciscans at most. She also wanted the young girls to fast, but they don't say what sort of abstinence she made a law for them. Saint Paula very much liked the literal sense of holy scripture. After her death, the bishops did her the honor or perhaps one should say the duty of carrying on their shoulder the body of her who had carried them all on her heart.[3]

The Blessed PAULA Malatesta, nun of Saint Claire. At least this one entered the convent only after leaving the temple of Hymen.

The Blessed PAULA of Montant, same. Like most virgins, to the extent one can be one in a convent.

Saint PAULINE. Like most saints; and Saint CANDIDA her mother.

Saint PELAGIA, virgin and martyr of Antioch. This girl, martyr of virginity and not of religion, had the courage to throw herself off a roof to avoid the brutality of her shameless judge. We are astonished, after this rare incident, to see the convent which bears her name serve as a retreat for Christian women whose conduct has not been quite the same as hers.

Saint PELAGIA, sinner and penitent, actress and reformer. The legend has connected this saint with a certain bishop, Saint Nennus, and celebrates his feast on the same day as hers; we will see why. Pelagia, whom the people of Antioch call "Marguerite" and "Pearl," was the star actress of this city and fulfilled the position with honor. Maximian, patriarch of Antioch, held a council; the assembled bishops, who thought all eyes were turned onto themselves, were scandalized that the grace and talent of this girl won more proselytes than their long beards did. They looked at her askance and perhaps could have done worse. But one of them, Nonnus, who knew a bit more about life, decided otherwise and managed so well that he converted Pelagia, so that at the same time she was exorcised, confessed, baptized, confirmed and communioned. Such it is to be pretty and well proportioned! Even the Church infringes its own rules and violates its own laws in order to favor beauty and charity.

Pelagia retired to the Mount of Olives, enclosed herself in a cell, and from time to time received the assistance of Nonnus, who made her pass for a eunuch; he had his reasons. When the good bishop felt himself no longer in condition to make the voyage, he sent a deacon to his penitent, who never left her without having "chanted tierce"[4] with her. She died in the middle of these holy exercises. The daughters of Val-de-Grâce claim to have some "relics of Pelagia." Serious authors have believed that Pelagia was the same as Saint Marguerite among the Greeks and Saint Marina among the Latins. See these two saints.

Saint PERPETUA. See Saint FELICITY.

Saint PERRONELLE or PETRONILLA, PERRINE, or PERNELLE, Roman virgin. We see, from the diversity of names, none of which is any better than the others, that we can't establish anything certain about the life of this saint. She is said to be the daughter of Saint Peter, because of the analogy of names: a strange manner of proving parenthood. But in the Church, everything is done in uncommon ways which would appear absurd if one "were not armed with the shield of faith."

Saint PERSEVERANDE, virgin. Not the patron of many girls.

Saint PHAINE, see Saint CLAUDE, or the seven octogenarian VIRGINS of Ancyra.

The Blessed PHILIPPA of Marnia. The life of this saint has nothing miraculous in it. She made the acquaintance of Francis of Assisi and his monks, embraced his rope belt and allowed herself to be directed by one Roger who was probably one of those "good-time Rogers."

The Blessed PHILIPPA de Medici, of the order of Saint Claire. This woman didn't inherit her family's taste for the arts. She buried herself in a convent and made herself famous by a nearly continuous silence. This circumstance of her life is as good as a miracle. The legendary, which we copy faithfully, adds, in order to give us an idea of her merit, that she never failed to help in the refectory except on the eve of her death.

Saint PHOEBE, deaconess of Cenchreae, disciple and hostess of Saint Paul.[5] The life story of this saint is contained in its title; it says everything. We add only one particularity that is little known, but good to know. It is that this holy woman made sure the apostle's letters reached their destination. I doubt that such a role would merit canonization today. The Phoebe of the pagans would not be charged with such commissions.

Saint PHERBULA, virgin and martyr &c. See TARBULA.

The Blessed PHILIPPINE of Châlons, of the order of Saint Claire. We only know the name of this nun, who lived toward the year 1440. If printing, which was discovered only ten years later, had been known then, we would doubtless have known more! It's a great loss for the city of Châlons!

The Blessed PIERRONE, PIRONE or PETRONILLA, tertiary of Immet-Werdeghem, near Mons in Hainaut. This nun offers nothing extraordinary except the strange name of her region.

Saint PHERBA.[6] Spiritual daughter of Saint Paul and originally from Corinth, this holy girl had a great deal of "charity." This last word explains everything. Saint Paul immortalized her in his correspondence with the Romans.

Saint POMPOSA, virgin, martyr, in Spain. This was a little madwoman. She went to insult her Mohammedan judge, who should not have had her decapitated but enclosed in his harem, if Pomposa was charming; if not, to put her among the slaves of those who were.

Saint POTAMIAN, virgin martyr of Alexandria. Chains, prisons, cauldrons of boiling tar on one side; virginity and the gospel on the other: that is the dilemma in which this courageous virgin was placed and which the Church proposes to modern girls. But times have changed and become more sophisticated. The boiling tar is in the mouth of nuns, to make their novices afraid. Virginity appears to have suffered the fate of currency: its value has declined for some time, and it's also true that for some time its specie has altered. As for the gospel, it's still spoken of.

Saint PROXEDE, Roman virgin. We send the reader, not without regret, to the article on Saint Marguerite, virgin and martyr. It serves for both of these imaginary saints.

Saint PUBLIA, widow, abbess of Antioch. This was an impertinent one who, every time Julian – described by fools as apostate – passed under the windows of her house where she ruled a little flock of virgins, affected to sing injurious psalms very loudly, such as this charitable and edifying verse: "May those who make idols resemble them." The first time the emperor heard them, he limited himself to ordering the girls to be quiet. They started up again even louder, encouraged by their old superior, Publia.

This recidivism displeased the philosopher prince, who had our widow administered several slaps by one of his guards, "from which she got very red cheeks" (as the legendary plainly adds). She went back to the house with the firm resolution to do worse than ever. It isn't known what became of her, but the Church obviously had to give her the title of martyr.

Saint PUDENTIANNE, Roman widow or virgin. Only the name of this saint is known, and perhaps she owes her cult to this clever silence.

Saint PULCHERIA, virgin empress; in Latin, AELIA PULCERIA. Probably the sanctity of Pulcheria is only gratitude on the part of the Church. This empress built temples and protected their ministers;

held councils; and, magnificently pious, hung on the sacred walls of the sanctuary a plaque loaded with jewels on which was written in large gold letters her vow of virginity.

Saint PUCINE. See her sister, Saint LINDRU.

RACHEL, see LEAH.

Saint RACHILDA, see Saint GUIBORAT.

Saint RADEGONDE,[1] queen of France and nun at Poitiers. Probably heaven erred in having Radegonde born into a royal family and in giving her a king as spouse, for Radegonde was born to be a nun. That's what the courtiers of her day called her, and it pleased fate that they were sincere. At twelve, our princess thought she saw in the gospel that virginity was recommended as a state of perfection and as the only way to happiness. At fifteen, she could have seen the contrary there with just as much basis. But as the legend says so well, "the Holy Spirit had spread more fire in her heart than light in her mind."

Consequently she enraged her husband who, when he wanted to approach his wife, only embraced a bundle of thorns; he felt himself rudely repulsed by a hair shirt, and encountered the stigmata-marks of Jesus everyplace where he would have wanted to imprint those of love. Clotaire was disgusted and sought in the arms of several mistresses what his wife let him take only with scolding. A more complaisant and less holy Radegonde could have prevented the disorders of her husband. From disgust Clotilde passed to hate, and the legend adds – doubtless for the edification of young spouses and to suggest a striking example for them – that the queen, far from working to bring her husband back, supported the feeling of alienation from her that he'd been forced to develop.

She did more; she even rejected the occasional returns of tenderness that this too good husband felt spring up in his heart, and she forced the bishops to ordain her deaconess and make her a nun. Radegonde finally came to the end of her enterprise. Nothing is impossible for a woman, especially when she is endowed with a holy obstinacy. Our readers will scarcely be able to understand how a young girl can continue to prefer to the throne and to the tender embraces of a vigorous spouse, a cloister, iron-pointed belts, etc. etc.

We were as surprised as our readers until we saw appear on the scene a certain Italian priest named Fortunatus, who didn't belie his name. He was a fine character; he made verses – Latin verses, true, but that was then the language of madrigals as well as of sacred chants. This Fortunatus, who was made a saint, served our saint as director, as ambassador, as secretary, as business agent; in a word, he served all the needs that a thirty-year old nun can have when overheated by fasting and excited by the frequent discipline that he also doubtless administered. Radegonde died in these mortifications of the flesh. The director wrote her biography and a defense of his penitent's life. No one could have firmer memories of it than he.

The Blessed RAINGARDE, widow and nun of Marsigny. After having given, in resignation, eight children to her husband, Raingarde thought she could think of herself and that it was time to retire from the world. The Blessed Robert of Arbrissel, that famous founder of Fontevrault, that severe reformer who, to mortify his flesh, regularly went to bed every night between two novice nuns whom he directed – Robert of Arbrissel, we say, by no means disapproved of Raingarde's plan; from the conjugal bed she passed to the cloister and died there. It might have been more glorious to die in the bed of honor, or on the field of battle.

RAHAB, courtesan in the city of Jericho.[2] This Old Testament saint was a rather bad citizen who harbored Jewish spies, enemies of her country. But it's God who permitted all that, in order to make a conqueror of his servant Joshua. Couldn't God have used a less vile instrument than Rahab to arrive at his goal? O altitudo!...

REBECCA, wife of the patriarch Isaac. We have found nothing in the life of this Old Testament saint, maturely examined, to justify a tradition which gives the nickname "Rebecca"[3] to ill-natured, quarrelsome women. It is true that this one imposed upon her husband, but it was so late in his life that she decided to fool him without thinking it was any crime.

Saints REDEMPTA, ROMULA, HERONDINE, Roman virgins. What to say about three spinsters who entered a convent fully alive and, having ceased to live, died there a long time afterward?

Saint REINE, virgin and martyr, from Alise in Burgundy in the diocese of Autun. We send the obliging reader back to Saint Marguerite. These two saints (says the severe Baillet) much resemble one another. In his own words he adds that "both were encountered by an Olibrius" who became their suitors, then their judges, and finally their executioners. That happens to others beside saints. Besides, hints the legend, the faithful from the diocese of Autun can't produce any better proof of the existence and sanctity of their patron than bones and ash. Unfortunately, the ash of Laïs[4] is the same as that of the Virgin Mary.

This good saint cures of disease those who have enough faith to believe in virgins.

Saint REINELDE or ERNELLE, virgin martyr in the region of Cleves; Latin REINILDIS and RAINILDIS. We will limit ourselves to reporting the circumstances of her martyrdom, which are curious. The Huns surprised her in a church between an underdeacon and a clerk. This situation didn't deter the barbarians, who, after having dragged her by the hair around the church, were happy to cut off her head.

Saint RENELLE, see Saint HERLINDA.

Saint RICTRUDE, widow and abbess. This saint deserves to be better known than many others, although she employed only very natural means to arrive at perfection. She was first a tender spouse and good mother. Widowed, she placed herself, it is true, under the direction of a saint, and died an abbess. This second part of her life got her altars in the Church; in society, they would be erected for the first part. Rictrude was from Gascony; we notice this because not many saints have come from that area.

Saint ROMAINE, see Saint BENEDICTA of Origny.

Saint ROMULA, see Saint REDEMPTA.

Saint ROSALIE. Offspring of Charlemagne, she didn't completely share his tastes. She liked to slip away from court to have little gatherings in the woods, preferring a throne of fern to the sparkle of a diadem. They have not placed her in the rank of virgins.

Saint ROSE of Peru, tertiary nun of Saint Dominic. If pagans in the ancient world made the blood of Christians flow, the Christians have amply paid them back in the new world against primitive idolaters.

Toward the year 1586 (when the Church had exhausted its supply of victims and began to look for new saints), Saint Rose was born in Lima, city of kings and capital of Peru in the heart of South America. Rose is the first saint of the new world. She was first called Isabelle, but the roses of her complexion gave her the present name. At the age of fifteen she felt that this nickname was a bit profane, so she lessened that in adding "Rose of Saint Mary." She took as her model the life of Saint Catherine of Siena (q.v.) and didn't do a bad job imitating her. She was struck by this moral and patriotic passage of the gospel: "Who wants to follow me shall leave mother and father."[5] To put it into practice, she took refuge for twenty years among the Dominicans.

Wouldn't her virginity have been just as secure under the maternal wings? Says the legend: "She was exercised by terrible temptations, which tormented her for fifteen years in a way that made her often fear that God might have abandoned her." The legend adds, to reassure us (and we needed it): "However, during all this time of trouble and warfare, only her imagination was wounded; her heart remained always invulnerable." Fine! We would like to believe it, but we will take the liberty of observing that once imagination is hurt, the heart is in great danger. She died at thirty-one years of age.

We hasten to warn virgins who are disposed to die such as they were born, and who will read us: we hasten to warn them that the example of Rose ought not to frighten them. It is more difficult to keep the vow of perpetual abstinence from pleasure when you are in Lima, a South American capital and city of sunshine, than in the convents of northern Germany.

Saint Hubert is invoked for rabies; Saint Roch is patron of the plague; Saint Leu cures fear; Saint Nicolas marries off girls and Saint Catherine boys; Saint Marguerite's belt helps produce handsome children, Saint Crispin good shoes; the rope belt of Saint Francis reconciles estranged spouses; water of Saint Genevieve cures eye disease. Alas! There is a disease more urgent, more widespread and of quite different consequence than rabies or plague, etc. This disease came to us from the country of Saint Rose. She ought to have asked heaven for the commission of presiding over the cure of this incurable and devastating disease.[6]

Saint ROSE of Viterbo, tertiary. This rose flowered for only eighteen springtimes, but our saint, at the age of three, had already resuscitated her aunt. She died in 1258 but her body, still virgin today in 1782, that is, for more than five hundred years, still conserves — says the reverend father Fulgence Ferot, Franciscan Recollect[7] — conserves as much freshness and "flexibility" as if it were full of life. The examination or the vote of a recollect in such a case is not suspect. These gentlemen are connoisseurs.

Saints RUFINA and SECONDA, Roman virgins and martyrs. These two virgins were engaged to be married when emperor Valerian started a new persecution against the sect of the Man-God or God-Man. Their future husbands, new Christians, wanted to abandon their religion, but not the women. Nothing more natural: Rufina and Seconda did the contrary. Nothing more edifying, but they paid with their lives, their faith violated. And nothing more just than their punishment, which the Church took for a martyrdom.

Saint RUSTILLA or MARCIA RUSTICULA, abbess of Saint Cesar in Arles. Nothing odd or even instructive in the life of this saint, who passed her entire life in a cloister and who was accused of meddling in profane affairs of government. She wasn't the only one.[8]

Saint SATURNINA. This virgin had her head cut off by her lover himself; he was furious to see that the good Jesus was preferred to him — as if the good Jesus were a rival to fear for long!

Saint SABINA, widow, and Saint SERAPIA, virgin, both martyrs. Serapia and Sabina were two good friends living together as closely as is possible for two women one of whom professes widowhood, the other virginity, and both Christianity. Their worship had been the occasion of their perfect intimacy. If they weren't saints, this intimate association could create violent suspicions, all the more since they lived in Italy during the second century of the Christian era.

Serapia was martyrized first. "Virilus," governor of Umbria (you have to admit that some unusual names are united here), made her appear before him and, to punish her, exposed her chastity in an ambiguous and shadowy place, as prey of starved Egyptians.

Serapia had a convenient system. She pretended that virginity is a virtue of the soul rather than of the body; and that this rose is conserved in all its freshness as long as the interior will doesn't go along with the external attack.[1] But we see that the poor virgin had little experience and that, if it takes a miracle to restrain two Egyptians in the presence of a girl who is abandoned to them, it takes another no less great to prevent this girl from sharing the pleasure revealed to her and which she grants in spite of herself to her resisting body. In this critical moment it isn't far from passive to active. But heaven pulled Serapia out of this jam. God permits the two Egyptians to fall into a stupor from which they only recovered (says the legend) after everyone was convinced that the virgin's chastity had won the victory.

If anyone accuses us of lacking intelligence, we will admit that this passage appeared obscure to us; we even thought we noticed that the sacred author wrote about torture to express in acceptable terms something that was scarcely acceptable. After this miracle — for miracle it was — Virilus had the head cut off of the one whom he'd not been able to deprive of a more precious treasure. Sabina, who couldn't live without her dear Serapia, joined her a year later in a similar martyrdom. Several hagiographers find no difficulty in giving Sabina the character of virgin, although she was a widow, and the legend gives a reason for this contradiction which still makes us smile. It could be (says the legend) that it was her association with Serapia that won her that title.

Saint SALOME, wife of the fisher Zebediah, mother of the apostles Jacob and John.[2] The presence of Jesus Christ caused the father to be abandoned by his two sons and by his wife, so that poor Zebediah was constrained to manage his boats and his nets alone — not without cursing, probably, the adventurer who took from him his pleasures and his support. Salome, the fisherman's wife, loved her children and, by this conduct, hoped to open a door to success for them. J.C. reprimanded her strongly for her ambition, which had its source in a mother's heart. That's what we know for sure about this saint, and posterity can manage without details that do no honor to the main hero.

Saint SAPIENCE, see Saint FAITH.

The Blessed SALOME, of the order of Saint Claire. Born in Russia, wed for twelve years to Coloman: to remain a virgin would do no honor to her august spouse. If only heaven had not meddled in their affairs. At her passing, her body distilled a curative oil. Fine!

The Blessed SANCHA, queen of Naples[3] and nun of Saint Claire. Wife of a king, sister-in-law of a saint and a bishop, founder of convents; what entitlement to be blessed!

SARA, wife of Abraham, mother of believers.[4] This "mother of those who believe" has no more children. As a "mother of those who see" she would have had many more. Without retracing the life that every good Christian knows, we will insist on only one point which does honor to the good nature and compliant character of this holy woman of ancient times. It is the kindness with which she urged her husband to sleep with her servant, no longer feeling herself in a condition to fulfill matrimonial duties. A good sermon could be made on this text, for modern spouses who still go to sermons.

The young SARA, wife of the young Tobias.[5] This young Sara was a terrible woman. She had already killed seven husbands on the wedding night. Young Tobias, who learned this circumstance, was nonetheless brave; the Lord's hand was with him and directed him, so that he didn't die like his predecessors, who probably weren't in a state of grace.

Saint SAVINA. This holy woman only went out at night, between dog and wolf, and often passed whole nights sighing on the tomb of martyrs. Her honor found its place there. We don't advise Christian virgins to visit churches so late at night, as she did.

Saint SCHOLASTICA. Nothing positive is known about this famous saint except that she visited her brother once a year. One evening, at the moment of separation, the saint ardently urged her brother, Saint Benedict, to spend the night together meditating on the joys of paradise. Saint Benedict excused himself, not wanting to sleep outside the convent. This saint had "principles." Scholastica insisted, but in vain; she was obliged to bring heaven into her cause. To do so, she stayed for a long time, elbows leaning on the table, and there came a storm, which obliged the father of the Benedictines to give his sister the satisfaction she had demanded. Soon afterward, Scholastica died, and her brother had the pleasure of seeing her soul fly to heaven in the form of a dove.

Perhaps it is in reading the Bible too much, or saints' lives, that modern philosophers have been tempted to become somewhat materialist.

Saint SECONDA or SECONDILLA, see Saint RUFINA.

Saint SEPTIMIA. Just like most saints.

Saint SIGOULEINE, widow, abbess of Triclar in Albigeois. A widow for twenty-two years, it was the fortunate bishop of Albi who received and consecrated her widowhood in his hands and ordained her deaconess.

Saint SOPHIA, see Saint FAITH.

Saint SOTERA, Roman virgin martyr. The martyrdom of this young virgin wasn't the cruellest a woman might endure, but certainly the most outrageous. Sotera was beautiful, and it was in the face that they struck her pitilessly. In those days they knew little about life.

The Blessed SERAPHINA. In the world, she was called Sueva. The anxieties of a bad household generated in her the vocation for the austerities of the cloister. We endure self-imposed pains more patiently than those imposed on us. And perhaps she had a few peccadilloes to expiate, for the legend reports that her husband accused her of adultery.

The Blessed MARIA SUARES of Toledo, nun of Saint Claire. Same as the Blessed Seraphina, except for the adultery accusation. She entered the convent only as a forty-one-year-old widow. It's a good age to be religious.

SUSANNA, Jewish woman at Babylon, Old Testament saint.[6] Susanna is the Bible's Lucretia. But to the degree that the Jewish people are inferior to the Roman people, to that extent is Susanna to Lucretia. Besides, who knows if Tarquin, placed next to two old men...and then this young Daniel who comes in right on time...For the rest, the Church demands only faith from us, and absolves us from all critical reason.

Saint SUSANNA, virgin martyr at Rome. The virginity and martyrdom of this Susanna are no better ascertained than the fidelity of the Jewish Susanna.

Saint STADIOLA. They burn incense to her in Berry as a virgin, although she was the mother of at least four children. She was the daughter of a bourgeois of Bourges. The good woman mortified her flesh all her life, preferring fresh-water fish to butcher's meat. She is invoked for rain and good weather. She is the Saint Genevieve of the Berrichons.[7]

Saint SYMPHROSE and her seven sons, martyrs at Tivoli near Rome. This widowed saint preferred to die and see her sons die than to keep a low profile and give in to the orders of her prince.

Saint SYNCLETICA, virgin. Born in Alexandria, Egypt, vowed herself to virginity (as was then the fashion, which hasn't come down to us) and had that in common with Saint Anthony, her contemporary. Almost all her life she combated "the most disturbing temptations." Saint Athanasius,[8] her biographer, doesn't add whether she always came out victorious. He says only that she died in the arms of angels that God sent to give her a foretaste of the joys of paradise. This is getting involved a bit late, one has to admit.

The Holy TABLE. It's not a saint. It's the altar where priests eat their daily bread and do... ...A host's table serviced by priests who for a reasonable price redeem their table companions; there couldn't be a lighter or costlier meal.[1]

Saint TATIANNE, see Saint MARTINA.

Saint TARBULA or PSERBUTHE, virgin, martyr, etc. It hasn't been confirmed whether this saint was tortured rather than martyred. They accused her of having poisoned the queen, wife of king Sapor of Persia. Thus religion seems to have counted for nothing in the story of her death. Without pausing over a fact, which isn't in our jurisdiction, since we are only writing the lives of saints and not of poisoners, we can dispense with informing our readers that when Tarbula was interrogated by the pontiff, or chief of the wise men, she won over her judge – more by her beauty than by her innocence – and brought him to propositions that our saint rejected, of course: an action equivalent to all the miracles she could have performed. The refused judge was thenceforth only her judge; our saint was condemned to be cut in two, which was done.

Saint TELURE, see the seven octogenarian virgins of Ancyra.

Saint THERESA DE JESUS, mother of the Carmelites of strict observance, reformer of the barefoot Carmelites. In 1515 Theresa was born at Avila in the kingdom of Castile in Spain. Her father had a dozen children from two wives: three girls, nine boys. Of all her brothers, Rodrigo de Cepeda inspired the most affection in our saint, who was born with very affectionate tendencies. The brother and sister were always together. Together they read the lives of saints and the adventures of Robinson Crusoe.² These books made the usual impression that they do on children. Theresa built, as they say, many castles in Spain. By and by she wanted to go on pilgrimage with her brother; by and by, when they played together, Theresa pretended to be the little nun and Rodrigo the little monk.

Theresa's mother loved romances and let her daughter read them; she, gifted with a lively imagination, took from them a particular taste. Theresa's mother was a flirt, and the daughter liked beautiful outfits, new fashions, etc. Into her mother's house came cousins a little older than Theresa, who related their follies to their cousin and perhaps made her do some of them. Beyond that, a certain relative, who visited the same house, managed to enflame with passion the heart of Theresa, which was already only too combustible.

Her mother died; her sister, a prude, replaced her and began by boarding out the little Theresa. They already had the mania, which still endures, of choosing convents as educational institutions for girls. It was there that Theresa's brain was set completely on fire. They made her read the work of Saint Jerome on virginity and the Alphabet of the Cordeliers of Ossuna; Theresa went mad. Add to this the revolts of nature awoken from the sleep of indifference. Cruel maladies suited to a forced continence succeeded in weakening her spirit and disposing it to all the pious reveries of the cloister.

Then there came upon her the need for a good director. She was (says our grand-uncle Baillet) twenty years in trying the terrain and sounding out confessors, without finding one who "understood her dispositions. Then she obtained from heaven the gift of tears, which was a great comfort to her for the moments when her soul was tormented by the aridity of contemplation. All her praying" (says the scholarly and penetrating Baillet) "was to represent to herself the humanity of Jesus." She rose as far as the prayer of "quietude" and sometimes to that of "union," that is, "to the simple enjoyment of God."

The irritating scarcity of good directors was still with her. A Dominican presented himself, but it wasn't his type of thing. This man was already in gallant exchange with other penitents, and he couldn't attend to everyone at once. Theresa rescued him from the charm he claimed to be under from a certain woman, and our saint went so far as to say that she couldn't "hold herself back from the too great facility she had in returning affection for affection, in this meeting." However, an attack of nervous illness put her an inch from ruin and caused much fainting. The masses she had said for her cure did nothing. She was saved only in taking Saint Joseph as her patron. Once cured, she devoted herself to hobbies, received many visits, and neglected mental prayer, for her spirit had become slave to the body. This happy intermission lasted some years.

When she returned to her original fervor, her sweet and divine Jesus returned his graces and favors, no longer hid from her caresses, and "appeared to her often in sensory and palpable forms." Then she took up the pen, and it is to these moments of ecstasy that we are indebted for the mystical writings that she has left: for example, "The Soul's Castle," which she composed at the order of the Carmelite Jerome Gratian whom she "esteemed" greatly. It was not with the consent of her director that she published "her thoughts on the Song of Songs. He judged that it was dangerous and a bad example that a woman should undertake to interpret this sacred book." For which we praise the confessor and the holy Inquisition which condemned the book and which ought to have placed on the Index[3] only this type of book. Theresa finally did something still more difficult than a good book. She reformed the Carms and died after this glorious and painful enterprise, sixty-seven years old.

She left the names Cepeda and Ahumada to take that of Jesus.

Saint THAÏS or TAÏSE, penitent. A celebrated courtesan of Egypt who professed both catinism and Christianity. These two conditions are perhaps not as heterogeneous as one might believe at first glance. Mary is both virgin and mother. Besides, what follows will prove our assertion.

Paphnutius, famous anchorite, felt a burning desire to convert this woman to himself and to the Lord. He donned a secular outfit and, not forgetting his purse, climbed up to Thaïs's place and paid in advance. Thaïs leads him into the chamber prepared for the amount. Paphnutius asks for one further removed; he had his plans. "Why?" said the future saint. "What are you afraid of, my friend? If it's people, I assure you no one will come in; if it's God, is there any place secret enough to hide from him? For a long time he has let me follow my profession and blesses it. Thanks to heaven, I haven't lacked anything so far."

The converter was converted. Edified by these sentiments, Paphnutius proposed that Thaïs follow him into his desert and sanctify her profession more especially in consecrating it to the service of ministers of the Lord. Thaïs, content with this prospect, judged his companions according to him, and through an impulse of grace consented to quit worldly society to turn herself over completely to the holy desires of Paphnutius, Saint Anthony, and Paul the Simple.

Saint THARSILLA, virgin, and Saint EMILIANA, aunts of Gregory the Great. The Blessed Gregory had three aunts, the two named above and a third who at first let herself be influenced by the example of her sisters — but not for long. Grace couldn't outweigh, in her heart, one of her valets whom she married. Destiny cannot be avoided; and if there are no more saints, it's not women who are to blame but the lack of grace.

Saint THEA of Palestine, see Saint VALENTINE.

Saint THELCHILDE or THEUTCHILDE, abbess of Jouane. It isn't known whether she was the sister of Saint Agilbert, bishop of Paris, or simply his very good friend. But what is certain is that, following the expressions of the legend, Thelchilde and the daughters of her community "conducted themselves like wise virgins, awaiting, in continual vigils, the celestial bridegroom, with lamps always lit and always supplied with oil."

Saint THECLA, virgin, first martyr of the Christian religion. Born in the first century of the Church, year 45, Thecla, still very young, was engaged to a meritorious young man. Two respectable families awaited with impatience the happy moment when they would be united. The Apostle Paul comes to Iconia. Thecla hears him;

right away she rejects the marriage, refuses the most urgent entreaties of her astonished parents, abandons her father's house, hides from mortal concerns and the tears of her lover, to follow Saint Paul and model her behavior on his. Such was the power of the gospel preached by this holy apostle.

Saint Gregory says – in a style more florid than one might expect from a father of the Church –, "Thecla joined myrrh with lilies." But while this phrase is pretty, it is unreliable and doesn't justify Saint Thecla. Her scorned lover had her pursued and delivered her into the hand of a judge, who condemned her to be torn apart by animals, a torture more deserved by the missionary who seduced her. She appeared nude in the amphitheater, but her innocence and purity (says the legend) covered the ignominy of her condition. Here the legend adds the usual clichés: the lions crouched at the saint's feet, heaven delivered her – no one knows how – from the stake which was to terminate the auto-da-fé of this "protomartyr" saint, that is, the first martyr of her sex.

We mean the first martyr of her sex on such an occasion, for before Thecla there doubtless were women martyred in other ways.

Saint THEODORA, Empress of the East.[4] Reading between the lines of praise in her biography, one glimpses an ambitious woman, who began by getting herself married to her sovereign, to the prejudice of another woman who was supposed to marry him. This other woman didn't lose her head. She got the emperor, Theodora's son, to force his mother to become a nun, along with her daughters. Theodora was thus a saint despite herself, for pious and zealous as she was in the dispute[5] about church images, she would have preferred the throne or the regency to the cloister.

Saint THEODORA, virgin of Alexandria and, as a consequence, Saint DIDYMUS, martyrs. This virgin, who resembles so many others offered by the legend and the world, would rather renounce her honor than her religion. Anyone who knows the feminine heart a little will not be surprised. Women have an imagination livelier than their senses.

Theodora got off with a good scare. Who doesn't know the story of this too fortunate saint? Who doesn't know how Didymus, one of her sect, disguised as a soldier, entered the place consecrated to the virginal martyrdom of Theodora; how our saint, not recognizing him at first, cowered in every corner of the chamber; how, reassured by the touching voice of Didymus, she found only a benefactor in him whom she had thought her executioner; how, finally, Theodora consented to the quid pro quo that the "fortunate" Didymus offered her, proved in advance all her gratitude, and thus eluded the judge's sentence.

There exists in the French theater a tragedy on this subject. But it should have been Molière, not Corneille,[6] who brought Saint Theodora to the stage!

Saint THEODORA, penitent. There is nothing miraculous in the life of this saint, and not much faith is needed to believe in her. She behaved with her husband pretty much as Mary with the good Joseph, only she didn't choose quite so well. So she felt obliged to do penance. To accomplish this praiseworthy plan, she dressed up as a man and stole away from her husband, to deliver herself completely to a whole convent of monks. Robert d'Arbrissel, for mortification, slept between two virgins; Theodora, to punish her conjugal infidelity, resigned herself to the good will of twenty monks. So she has her altars and, above all, her imitators.

Saint THEODOSE or THEODOSIA, virgin and martyr at Caesarea in Palestine. Like most martyrs.

Saint THEODOTE and her children, martyrs in Bithynia, same.

Saint THEONILLA, same again, or see Saint DOMNINA.

Saint THERACIA. Like most saints.

The Holy TRINITY. It isn't the name of a saint, but one is sainted only so far as one believes in the power of this word, which in itself is only a reheated serving of the famous "ternary" number of ancient Greek metaphysicians.

U·V·Y·Z

Saint VALBURGE, German. This is one of those saints for whom one could write an all-purpose life; that is to say, she fasted, sang psalms, yawned, groomed herself, recruited virgins, and died as useful to herself as to the world which lost her without noticing and which invokes her without knowing her.

Saint VALERIE, martyr, wife of Saint Vital, also a martyr. We know practically nothing of these martyrs except their names — but that suffices to be saints.

Saint VALENTINE & her companion Saint THEA, virgins and martyrs, in Palestine. These were two hussies who, without respecting people's rights, and driven by a zeal worse than indiscreet, kicked over an altar of the Roman gods and drew on themselves a punishment that was just albeit too cruel, which the Church judged suitable to qualify as martyrdom.

Saint VALTRUDE or VAUDRU, patron of Mons in Hainaut. After having four children with her husband, she managed to persuade him to the monastic life. As for our saint, she remained in the world, had visions, exposed herself to the gossip and sarcasm of her neighbors, and finally retired into a cloister herself. Our grand-uncle says that there were the most mortifying contradictions to wipe away, not on the part of others but on hers: "Phantasms suggestively dared to attack her chastity." She died in pain and was consequently beatified and canonized.

N.B. This article was edited when someone sent us the following correction. We will always make it a duty and a pleasure to sacrifice our pride to the truth.

Saint VALTRUDE, spouse of Saint Vincent, called Mauger or Madelgaire, and mother of four children. Items justifying the sanctity of this woman are lacking for the hagiographer, but a mother of four children has no need of further titles to merit a grain of incense; and here we will praise the spirit and the behavior of the Church of the Low Countries, this blessed woman's homeland, for having given a place in its calendar to the fecund spouse of the good Vincent Mauger. One can't too strongly encourage marriage between honest people. The husband of Valtrude founded two monasteries. We will admit, with our usual veracity, that this is to destroy with one hand what one has made with the other. But our saint wasn't one for nothing. They even say that if she had been believed, rather than burden the earth with two more convents, the good Vincent would have brought into the world two more little saints. But apparently Mauger was suited by then only to pious foundations.

Saint VERONICA. The pious reader will know that "Veronica" is not a saint's name. This word comes from "vera icon" or "iconica," which means a true image or representation. The people call her the "Holy Face" of Jesus Christ. These sorts of misunderstandings and transpositions are frequent in the Bible and in the legend. Devotion is not always as bright as it is fervent.

Saint VICTORIA, martyr. The legend, which doesn't willingly keep silent, says almost nothing about her, but we are no less obliged to furnish candles to burn on the altar of this unknown saint.

Saint VICTORIA, Roman virgin, see Saint ANATOLIA, her sister.

Saint VICTORIA, martyr under the Vandals, see Saint DATIVE.

The holy VIRGINS and martyrs under the Vandals. Huneric, king of the Vandals, hated Christian virgins, so he ordered his soldiers to rape them, which their bishops (he said) would obtain from them without effort; and he was punctually obeyed. These virgins thus visited by the Vandals were no longer good for anything but to be saints; and so they were indeed.

Saint URSULA and her companions, virgins and martyrs, commonly called the eleven thousand VIRGINS. Eleven thousand virgins!... Certainly the book in which such marvels are found is justly called *The Golden Legend*! As it is said: "the fabled time of the age of gold." Eleven thousand maidens!...But at the same time, how irritating that the legend hasn't kept their names for us! How irritating that it has left us no certain monument of such an interesting story as that of the martyrdom of eleven thousand virgins!

Cologne, privileged city forever famous, you were the glorious theater of this prodigy. It is within your walls that these eleven thousand virgins were born and died![1] Teach us what influence you could have had, to enclose so many treasures! Alas, in our day Rome, Paris and London all together would furnish scarcely a decimal fraction of that number....

Friend reader, come back a moment from your rightful surprise, and don't allow yourself to be seduced, as we were, by the first lines on a page. This number of eleven thousand – if we are to believe several scholars such as Sirmond, Valois, etc. – is only a single person named "Undecemilla": a name which the scribes, either maladroit or lovers of miracles, metamorphosed and frenchified into "onze mille." "Undecimilla," though very rare and perhaps unique, is, however, no less natural a name, according to the scholars just cited, than "Decimilla," "Septimilla," "Sextilla," "Quintilla," "Quartilla," etc., of which there are various examples.[2] Other scholars, more indulgent and less bold, give simply eleven companions to the virgin Ursula. And eleven is a perfectly reasonable number, since Boileau[3] reduced to three the number of intact women. Besides, "Non nobis inter eos tantos componere lites."[4]

The seven octogenarian VIRGINS of Ancyra, see Saint CLAUDE.

Saint VILORADE, see Saint GUIBORAT; they are the same.

The Blessed VIRIDIANA, tertiary. She always wore a belt – not that of the graces. But born in Tuscany, she had desires to combat, and she needed nothing less than a circle of iron to chastise the demon of the flesh during the forty-two years that she remained enclosed in a cell and was visited only by Francis of Assisi. From him she received the habit and the rope belt.

Saint ULPHE, from Picardy. It seems that this saint had the misfortune to be attractive, for to get rid of her suitors and to remove from her spouse, Jesus, any subject for jealousy if she should allow any of his rivals near her, she scratched her face to bits; and to justify this action she pretended to be insane. She must not have had much trouble pretending. She tore out her hair, covered herself in mud, and through the power of uncleanliness finally made herself worthy of her divine husband.

This fine deed completed, she goes into the desert where, after fifty years of penitence, she thought (a bit late, it's true) of giving a motive to her penitence. A hermit, "chaste as an angel," met her and (this old spinster being the first woman he had ever seen) thought it was the devil's trap. The good old man didn't know any better; he didn't know that the demon doesn't inhabit filth-ridden fifty-year-old bodies. One surprising thing is that she was able, through her example, to get the girls of Amiens to make a vow of virginity, as she had done. But this deed will become more believable if it allows them each to have another Saint Domitus.

She performed miracles, as is ordinary for saints. Here is one that proves how good and indulgent the good God is toward us sinners. One day Saint Domitus, the very good friend of Saint Ulphe, called to his dear penitent as she passed by his cell. The frogs were croaking loudly at that moment and covered the holy hermit's voice. Apparently she didn't hear him, and he scolded Saint Ulphe for not having run to his voice. Saint Ulphe, stricken, begged the Lord to make all the frogs silent in the local marshes. God said: Let the frogs be silent, and the frogs were silent. People assure us that they still are silent; when I go to Amiens I shall verify this important fact.

Ulphe died, not in the ordinary way in the arms of her director, but in those of a good friend of her type.

I extended myself a bit on this saint because she was recommended to me.

Saint URSULA. We won't say anything about her; she is the patron of messieurs the doctors of the Sorbonne.

Saint YMME, see Saint AME or AMEE.

Saint YSOIE, see Saint EUSEBIA; they are the same.

Saint ZOE, wife of a court registrar, martyr at Rome. For six years Zoe was mute. Saint Sebastian gave her back her speech, whether miraculously or naturally. Grateful for a benefit so important for herself and her sex, Zoe wanted to be a martyr of a religion that made mute women speak. She was hanged. Isn't this a case of the gratitude surpassing the benefit?

APPENDIX

GENEVIEVE STANZAS

The stanzas from "Genevieve" are full of double entendres, puns, and erotic symbolism, much of which can't be translated with a single word or phrase. For example, the opening phrase "en diligence" might mean "with all due haste," or "conscientiously," or "in [the type of carriage called] a diligence." The word "indulgence" might have an erotic or a religious meaning, as might many others used in the verse. The result is a densely textured, playful and subversive paean to erotic love, parodying the vocabulary of religious devotion as had been done since the days of Provençal troubadours and Italian stilnuovisti. Capital letters of the title are in the original, and we may note that the verse form is not what we would now mean by "couplets" but refers rather to the stanzas of a song.

COUPLETS IMPIES
Addressés à une aimable veuve, qui avoit Geneviève pour patrone

Courez en diligence,
Trop crédules Badauts!
Pour gagner l'Indulgence
Que l'on prodigue aux Sots.
D'une autre Geneviève
Nos coeurs se sont épris,
Qui nous feroit mieux qu'Eve
Chasser du Paradis.

De Paris la Patrone
Est vierge, nous dit-on.
Cependant on lui donne

Marcel pour Compagnon.
Même champ les rassemble
Auprès de leurs moutons;
Mais étoient-ils ensemble
Toujours en oraisons?

Choisis donc, ainsi qu'elle,
Un Compagnon d'amour.
Prends-la pour ton modèle;
Tu feras Sainte un jour.
L'almanach de Cythère
Fera place à ton nom;
À veuve qui fait plaire
On a dévotion.

À ta Chapelle sainte
Avec zèle on ira;
Dans son étroite enceinte
Un cierge on brulera.
De nos Vierges tremblantes
Geneviève est l'appui,
De nos Veuves souffrantes
Tu calmeras l'ennui.

CHRONOLOGY

1750 August 15: Pierre Sylvain Maréchal born into the Catholic family of a Parisian wine-merchant.

1770s Maréchal publishes pastorals or "bergeries" and other poetry; studies law; participates in literary salons; begins work at the Mazarin Library.

1776 British colonies in the new world declare independence; France's support to the rebel Americans against its commercial and colonial archrival, England, overburdens its treasury.

1780 Maréchal collaborates with the engraver F.-A. David on *Antiquités d'Herculanum*.

1788 Maréchal publishes his *Almanach des honnêtes gens*, which is publicly burnt; he is jailed for several months.

1789 May 5: The Estates-General opens at Versailles in order to resolve the financial crisis; this is its first meeting since 1614.
June 20: The Tennis Court Oath: deputies from the third estate (middle classes), with some clerics, swear not to disband until they produce a constitution. Excluded from the usual assembly hall, they meet in the indoor tennis court or Jeu de Paumes, constitute themselves a National Assembly representing the nation, and begin work on a Declaration of the Rights of Man and the Citizen, published in August. Women are not enfranchised.
July 14: Citizens searching for arms take the Bastille, a fourteenth-century fortress and a prison for counterfeiters, "dangerous"

authors such as the Marquis de Sade, and other adversaries of the monarchy.
August 4: The National Assembly abolishes feudal privileges and obligations.
October 5–6: Market women lead a march to Versailles to bring the king, Louis XVI, back to Paris with wagonloads of grain.
November 2: Nationalization and confiscation of Church property.

1790 February: Eighty-three departments of France created from previous provinces.
May 21: National Assembly creates forty-eight sections of Paris. Their autonomy and popular sovereignty generate conflict with the national government over the next three years; they are eventually replaced by the arrondissement system.
Publication of *Nouvelle légende dorée*. Maréchal works as editor of the well-known journal *Révolutions de Paris*.

1791 June 20–21: The royal family flee Paris, are caught at Varennes before they can cross the border into Austrian Belgium. Later, Louis is forced to ratify the new constitution; the new government is renamed the Convention.
September 27: Emancipation of France's Jews into full citizenship.

1792 Maréchal marries Marie-Anne Desprès.
April: France declares war on Austria. Delegations of women demand full citizenship rights at the National Assembly.
"La Marseillaise" composed by Captain Rouget de Lisle; in 1795 it becomes the national anthem.
August 10: Parisian insurrection demanding dethronement; a new city government, the Commune of Paris, is created; Convention suspends monarchy after Louis vetoes Convention decrees. Royalism becomes a capital offense; the royal family are made virtual prisoners.

September 2–4: Massacre of about 1100 noble and clerical "suspects" in prisons and convents by Parisians, some en route to join the army.

September 20: Divorce, free and on demand, made law. It would be banned again in 1816.

September 22: The Convention proclaims the Republic; this becomes the beginning of Year I of the new revolutionary calendar.

1793 January 21: Execution of Louis XVI after trial for treason.

February 1: War declared on England and Holland; in March, on Spain. Food riots in Paris; ongoing revolts in some regions amounting to civil war.

April 6: The Convention creates a Committee of Public Safety, a war dictatorship to eliminate counter-revolution, raise armies and regulate the economy. Its regime is called "the Terror." Maximilien Robespierre becomes its dominant figure after July.

September: The Terror officially declared; due process suspended for anyone suspected of actual or potential subversion of the government; price controls decreed for foodstuffs.

October 16: Execution of the queen, Marie-Antoinette.

October 18–February 20: Maréchal's play *Le jugement derniere des rois* produced at the Théâtre de la République.

October 30: Robespierre orders all women's political clubs dissolved, establishes rules for female dress; public execution of leading moderates.

November 10: Festival of Reason. Paris churches closed to worship. Resistance to the government continues, especially in the north-west and south-east.

December 8: The former Marquis de Sade, who had renounced his title and privileges and had held official positions in the revolutionary Paris sections, arrested as an enemy of the Republic. Powers of the Paris sections curtailed as threats to the war effort; all civil powers centralized in the Committee of Public Safety.

CHRONOLOGY

1794   February 4: Abolition of slavery in the French Caribbean colonies.
February 28: Last issue of *Révolutions de Paris*.
June 8: Festival of the Supreme Being. Atheism defined as counter-revolutionary.
July 28: Execution of Robespierre, end of the Terror, beginning of the reaction called "Thermidorean" after the revolutionary name for this month, Thermidor.
October 13: Sade freed from prison.

1795   April–May: Parisians invade government meetings to protest famine, unemployment and inflation; the uprisings are suppressed by the army.
June 27: A royalist invasion is defeated.
August: all political clubs are dissolved.
September: A new constitution postpones universal suffrage, legitimizes rule of the elite. The new government is called the Directory.
November: After release from prison, François-Noel ("Gracchus") Babeuf forms a club to agitate for overthrow of the Directory, for return to the (suspended) 1793 constitution, for land redistribution, and for development of genuine equality.

1796   March: Maréchal joins the "secret directorate" of Babeuf's group to plan the insurrection; he writes songs and a Manifesto for the movement. Napoleon Bonaparte appointed commander of the French army in Italy.
May 10: Babeuf and others in the "Society of Equals" arrested on the eve of their planned insurrection through betrayal by an agent. Maréchal escapes arrest.

1797   May 27: Babeuf executed by guillotine.

1798   July: Napoleon lands in Egypt, plans an invasion of England but abandons the idea.

1799 November 9: A coup overthrows the Directory, replaces it with three consuls and a new constitution, establishes Napoleon as First Consul; he declares, "The revolution is over."

1801 Maréchal publishes his novella, *La femme abbé*; his study of Hebrew and Christian scripture, *Pour et contre la Bible*; and his *Projet* listing reasons why women should not learn to read.

1802 Napoleon sends armies to the colonies to re-establish slavery; they are defeated by the Haitian army under General Dessalines, a freed slave, but in Guadeloupe slavery would last until 1848.

1803 January 18: Maréchal dies at home of natural causes, attended by his wife and friends.

1804 May 18: Napoleon has himself proclaimed Emperor, in the presence of the Pope.

NOTES

DEDICATORY EPISTLE...

1. Baillet: The relationship is metaphorical, not literal, for Baillet (1649-1706), a scholarly rationalistic priest and librarian to a Parisian nobleman, compiled several volumes on saints and ecclesiastical history. His major hagiographical collection, organized as a calendar, offers much to create doubt, even to parody. Maréchal doesn't specify which of Baillet's works he used, but this collection would certainly have been among them. Noailles (1651-1729) was a cardinal and archbishop of Paris.
2. displacer: The French is "dénicheur" from the verb "dénicher," literally to throw a bird out of its nest. There is a pun with the niche or recessed spot in which statues of saints often stood in a church.
3. faith: Various possible biblical sources, e.g., 2 Kings 1:3, 6; Matt. 8:10; Luke 7:9.

A

1. amusing: "Genou" is French for "knee," and "genitor" is Latin for "procreator."
2. Berry: a region in central France. Its "Antiquities" would be a volume or set of volumes describing its Roman and medieval remains.
3. not enough: There are degrees of holiness. A full saint has been canonized in an ecclesiastical process developed by the Church bureaucracy in the eleventh century, and his or her veneration is binding on every Catholic. A "blessed" person, beatified but not

canonized, may be venerated at some times and places but not necessarily by every Catholic. Thus many of Maréchal's saints are what he calls "semi-saints."

4. vapors: depression, hysteria or moodiness, thought to be caused by exhalations from the stomach or other internal organ rising to the brain.
5. intendants: functionaries under the old regime, with royal authorization and unlimited powers in police, justice, and financial jurisdictions.
6. Pallas: Pallas Athena is the Greek goddess of wisdom. Priapus is a phallic deity. Below, Maréchal adds Diana, goddess of virginity.
7. in 1789: New vows were made illegal in 1790; Maréchal invokes the start of the revolution rather than the date of the actual law.
8. scapular: a short cloak covering the shoulders.
9. penitential shirt: an undergarment made of any rough material, worn in order to "mortify the flesh."
10. Ampoule: the vial of holy oil said to have been brought from heaven by a dove for the baptism of Clovis into Catholicism about 499.
11. Clotaire III, Merovingian king of Neustria (657–673); his father, Clovis II, ruled from 639 to 657.
12. Third-order men and women, or tertiaries, are lay persons whose devotion to (and, often, financial support of) a particular order, convent or cleric earns them special privileges such as private confession or consultation, wearing the order's garment or insignia, etc. Many of Maréchal's saints are tertiaries.
13. the good old times: The ironic revolutionary phrase for the pre-revolutionary few centuries.
14. Ane: the word means "ass" (donkey) in French.
15. apostle: Paul, in Rom. 11:33. "Altitudo" can mean either height or depth and expresses wonder or exaltation (sardonically, with Maréchal).
16. good cause: The Carmelites' foundational myth linked them with the prophet Elijah, who was thought to have foretold the coming of the messiah (Jesus); thus Marian devotion was characteristic of the order.

17. presented to old Simeon: Luke 2:36-38.
18. The story of Hannah (Anna or Anne), Samuel's mother, is told in 1 Sam. 1.
19. ceremony: Peter Abelard (1079-1142), priest and radical theologian, was castrated by agents of the canon Fulbert, uncle of Héloïse, the Parisian girl whose tutor and lover Abelard had been before their clandestine marriage. The practice of creating eunuchs by castration was considered "Asiatic."
20. Jerome: (about 347-420), born in what is now Croatia; theologian and polemicist, spiritual advisor, translator of the Hebrew Bible into Latin and parts of the Christian Bible from Greek into Latin; the whole called "Vulgate" because Latin was the vernacular in Rome and its empire.
21. energumens: excited, intense persons.
22. bacchantes: woman followers of the demi-god Bacchus, whose worshipers might engage in orgiastic or violent behavior.
23. Capet: (938-996), founder of the dynasty that ruled France to 1328.
24. "Essay on Monachism": Maréchal does not supply an author's name for this essay.

B

1. converse: a layperson who lives in a convent or monastery to do penance or renounce the world but who is not actually a nun or monk; he or she would perform domestic services or manual labor for the institution.
2. him: Although Maréchal often specifies "lecteure," woman reader, here the word "lecteur" and the grammar indicate that the man reader is intended or included.
3. Graces: the three Graces – Aglaia, Thalia and Euphrosyne, daughters of Zeus – personified beauty and charm; they form a well known motif in classical and later art.
4. Beguines: devout laywomen who formed urban communities, lived on the sale of their handicrafts, and performed charitable works.

5. Berenice: a third-century BCE queen who dedicated her hair to Venus for the safe return of her husband, Ptolemy III, from a war; legend claimed that the hair was transformed into a star or comet.
6. step-mother: a second wife might be expected to protect her prospective inheritance and that of her own children by preventing the marriage of her husband's offspring from the first marriage and the proliferation of heirs; hence the "wicked stepmother" figure, grounded in economic reality.
7. Saint Louis: Louis IX (1215-1270), king of France. During his reign, France won Normandy and other territories from England and made Henry III of England his vassal as duke of Aquitaine. He led a crusade to Egypt, was imprisoned in Syria, built the Sorbonne and other important buildings in Paris, and died en route to Tunis for another crusade. His mother had ruled for some years as regent.
8. Americans: indigenous peoples of the Americas. Albigensians: a religious sect in the region of Albi, southern France. Also known as Cathars, they were considered heretics by the Roman Catholics and were exterminated in a long intermittent war culminating in the seizure of their citadel-fortress, Montségur, in 1244.
9. Thaumaturge: Greek for "Wonder-worker."
10. Media: ancient Iran.
11. Cana: cf. John 2:1-11.

C

1. Petites-Maisons: a lunatic asylum.
2. name: "celer" is Latin for "speedy."
3. modern: Chantal was beatified in 1751 and canonized in 1767.
4. Marsollier: Jacques Marsollier (1647-1724) wrote a biography of St. Francis de Sales, as well as a volume on various lands, taxes and other temporal goods of the Church.
5. Cadière: In 1731, a middle-class girl, Marie-Catherine Cadière, sued her spiritual director, the Jesuit Father J.-B. Girard, for sexual molestation over a period of two years, 1728-1729. He had

impregnated her and personally given her an abortion. Mlle. Cadière suffered epileptic convulsions during much of this time. Father Girard was acquitted. The trial records of this notorious case were published in French and in English (cf. DeToledo), and generated ballads and obscene novellas for decades.

6. Lucretius: Roman poet, c. 99 BCE-55 BCE; his *De rerum naturae* (*On the Nature of Things*) is a long, rationalistic poem on science and morality. Maréchal omits the last word of the sentence: So strong was religion in persuading [to evil deeds: *malorum*].
7. odor: one of the signs of sainthood was said to be a fragrant odor emanating from the corpse.
8. mitre: a bishop's tall, arch-shaped headdress.
9. joker: doubtless Maréchal himself.
10. Portiuncula...modest: the suffix is a diminutive, so the meaning is "a small share" or "small portion."
11. Clovis: (465-511), Merovingian king of the Franks, baptized about 498 by St. Rémi at Reims and thus the first Christian ruler of France (Gaul, at the time).
12. *Golden Legend: Legenda Aurea*, the massive hagiographical collection compiled about 1260 by Jacob Voragine, Dominican administrator and later archbishop of Genoa. The collection combined many sources of the previous millennium. This is whence Maréchal derives his title, though he used many other sources as well, so that when he writes "the legend" he might have any version before him. Clotilde has no legend of her own in Voragine.
13. Capucine: one of the independent Franciscan orders, founded about 1525 as a preaching and missionary order. The name refers to the hood (Italian: cappuccio) that was a distinctive part of their habit (uniform).
14. marries them off: provides a dowry for the daughter of a poor family.
15. Not everyone: a pun on the saint's name and that of the Greek city, which was a center of wealth and lechery in the classical period; also (in French) a possible sexual innuendo with "s'élever": to rise up, mount, get excited, etc.
16. Henry: Henry II, Holy Roman Emperor, 1002-1024.

D

1. Julian: Roman emperor (361-63) who accepted, then abandoned, Christianity and issued an edict of religious toleration.
2. Vandals: Germanic tribe that invaded Gaul (406), Spain (409), and northern Africa (429). Although Christians, they were not of the Roman Catholic variety. In 533 the Romans reconquered northern Africa, and the Vandals disappeared as a political force.
3. *"Te Deum"*: opening words of a well known Latin hymn of thanks, used ironically here to describe the Jewish victory psalm in Judges 5 where, with Judges 4:12-24, this story is told. Maréchal errs in the detail of strong drink, for Jael offers only milk (although Judith, in a similar tale, does give wine).
4. Oda of Savoy was the wife of Bishop Arnoul of Metz during the seventh century, before clerical celibacy was made an official Church rule.
5. Attila: (d. 453), leader of the Huns, an Asiatic tribe; invader of central Europe, Gaul and Italy, with a reputation for brutality.

E

1. Thorn, sponge: In French, "épine" and "éponge", items mentioned in the story of Jesus's passion (suffering) in Matt. 27:27-54, Mark 15:16-39.
2. Diocletian: Roman emperor (284-305) of humble Yugoslavian birth.
3. the gift of tongues: See Acts 2:1-4 and 10:44-46.
4. mother: Maréchal does not supply the mother's name.

NOTES

F

1. Constantine: (about 288-337), Roman emperor who converted to Christianity and issued an edict saying that it would be tolerated throughout the empire.
2. Montanism: a second-century enthusiastic (ecstatic) Christian sect centered in Asia Minor.
3. Abraham is instructed by God to sacrifice his son, Isaac: Gen. 22:1-24.
4. Collatines: an order founded in the early fifteenth century, its name probably derived from the Roman area in which it was located.

G

1. Symmachus: (about 345-405), Roman orator and administrator.
2. Bollandists: a group of Belgian Jesuits named after a seventeenth-century leader and editor, Jean Bolland. They were commissioned by the Vatican to produce an authoritative edition of saints' lives consulting all sources and calendrically arranged. Their volumes, the *Acta Sanctorum*, extending into October saints by 1789, would have been among Maréchal's sources.
3. "lambs": seals blessed by the pope and stamped with the image of a lamb.
4. candle: in some illustrations, Genevieve is shown with a long, white candle representing one of her minor miracles. Maréchal, certainly the author of the stanzas, uses allegorical symbolism long familiar (e.g., from the ending of Jean de Meun's thirteenth-century *Roman de la Rose*), and used it in other songs known or believed to be by him (e.g., "Une fin" in Marion, 140-41).
5. this profane name: Gorgons were three sister-monsters of ancient Greek myth, with hideous faces and snakes for hair; they turned to stone anyone who met their gaze.
6. Jason: hero of ancient Greek myth who had to recover a stolen golden ram's fleece. Maréchal has attributed to Jason the eleventh

of Hercules' twelve labors: to acquire the golden apples of the Hesperides, which were guarded by a dragon. The reader may decide whether this error is inadvertent or deliberate, serving a sexual innuendo.
7. name: In Latin, "gula" means "gluttony," one of the seven deadly sins.

H

1. Hymen: ancient Greek personification of marital sex.
2. *Quot sunt Presbyteri...*: However many priests were there, that's how many masses she chose to have.
3. Calvary: place near Jerusalem where Jesus is said in Luke 23:33 to have been crucified; other gospels refer to the place as Golgotha.
4. Bernard: (1090-1153), theologian and preacher, founder and abbot of the Cistercian house at Clairvaux, advisor to popes. Hildegarde's visionary writings were examined by the bishop and clergy of Mayence (Mainz), to a favorable verdict. Mont Saint-Robert is Rupertsburg, near Bingen.

I · J

1. Dagobert: Dagobert II, Merovingian king (d. 679).
2. Charlemagne: (c. 742-814), Carolingian king and, from Christmas Day 800 when he was crowned by the pope, Holy Roman Emperor. The dynasty is named for him, though founded by his father, Pepin the Short. In addition to many military conquests, Charlemagne presided over a courtly "cultural renaissance."
3. Annunciad: a religious order at Bourges founded by Jeanne de Valois (1464-1505). The name refers to the angelic announcement made to Mary (the "Ave Maria" or "Hail Mary") regarding her conception of Jesus.
4. *res miranda*: Latin, a thing to be wondered at.
5. *monitum*: Latin, admonition, warning.

NOTES

6. Judith: The Book of Judith is not found in all Bibles because it is considered apocryphal, i.e., among those not included in the Palestinian Hebrew Bible because not believed to be divinely inspired and thus canonical. However, the apocryphal books were added to the Greek translation of the Hebrew Bible (the Septuagint, about 200–250 BCE) made by Alexandrian Jews who included works popular in their city. This Greek translation, rather than earlier Hebrew or Aramaic texts, was accepted as authoritative despite the existence of other, more accurate translation by Jews of their scripture. St. Jerome coined the word "apocryphal" (hidden) when he translated scripture from Hebrew into Latin after about 383 CE.

L

1. Tear: In French, "larme." This would most likely be a tear of the sorrowing Virgin Mary.
2. Leah, Rachel, and Jacob: See Gen. 29:16 ff.
3. Jacob's rod: a plant, perhaps asphodel or ragwort ("herbe de S. Jacques").
4. Canaanite woman: perhaps from 1 Chron. 2:3 or Gen. 38:2.
5. Tyre, on the coast of what is now Lebanon, is not the same as Thyatira, Lydia's home town in the Turkish region also called Lydia. Paul met Lydia in the Macedonian city of Philippi, where he baptized a group of Jewish women who supported him generously; cf. Acts 16:13-15.

M

1. Othon: (32–69 CE), Roman emperor who committed suicide.
2. anchorites: man or woman hermits enclosed in cells. Some lived in the desert, but in European or English cities the cell would likely be built onto a church wall; the anchorite would be supported at church and municipal expense, offering in return spiritual guidance and prayers.

NOTES

3. Alaric: Alaric I (370-410), king of the Germanic nation called the Visigoths, besieged Rome several times between 408 and 410.
4. Ambrose: (340-397), bishop of Milan, theologian preacher, Roman administrator.
5. Ferot: Ferot published a Franciscan legendary a decade earlier than Maréchal's; Hyacinth was canonized in 1807, after Maréchal died, so at the time of writing she was only a "semi-saint," or "blessed."
6. *lex talionis*: equivalent justice or retaliation: "eye for eye, tooth for tooth," cf. Exod. 21:24-25, Deut. 19:21.
7. queen of Scotland: queen consort of Malcolm III, Marguerite died in 1093; she founded monasteries and performed charitable works.
8. Ovid: (43 BCE-18 CE), celebrated Latin poet whose erotic works were well known down the ages, as was his epic myth collection, the *Metamorphoses*.
9. massacre: On August 24, 1572 – feast day of St. Bartholomew – French Protestants (Huguenots) gathered in Paris for a royal wedding and were massacred by Catholics. This began another battle in the series of civil wars that had already gone on for a decade and that continued for another twenty years until the Edict of Nantes (1598) granted freedom of worship and allowed Protestants the right to establish churches. In 1685, Louis XIV revoked the Edict.
10. Phebus: Greco-Roman figure of Apollo, patron deity of poetry, music and oracles.
11. *Lassata...*: exhausted by men, not satiated; part of line 130 in Juvenal's Satire VI, on women; this line refers to Messalina, a Roman empress.
12. sirens: mythical sea-creatures in Homer's *Odyssey*, whose song tempts sailors onto the rocks.
13. Charybdis, Scylla: two more dangers in the *Odyssey*; the former a whirlpool, the latter a monster that devoured sailors. Maréchal seems to have mixed them up.
14. delivered from the tyranny of the flesh: The allusion is probably to menopause.

15. catinism: prostitution; derived from a slang word for a prostitute.
16. Adonis: in Greek myth, a beautiful youth desired by Aphrodite the goddess of erotic love, and killed by a boar while hunting.
17. Argus: a mythical herdsman with eyes all over his body.
18. spot on his forehead: the reference here may be to the sign of cuckoldry: horns or bumps sprouting on the deceived husband's forehead.
19. Origen: (about 185-254 CE), Egyptian theologian, ascetic and preacher, who castrated himself to avoid sexual temptation. Some of Origen's theories were controversial; Rufinus, a follower of Origen, was denounced by Jerome.
20. Augustine: (354-430), bishop of Hippo in north Africa, theologian, author of *Confessions*, *City of God*, and many other seminal works of doctrine and polemic.

N · O

1. nasty transposition: perhaps because Nicerates, a politician in ancient Italy, killed his wife and committed suicide.
2. Naz: short for Nazianzen (330-390), theologian and bishop of Constantinople.
3. These two words...astonished: a nymph was a mythical Greek personification of a natural object (tree, stream, etc.), usually represented as young, beautiful, and naked, and not always chaste.
4. harpies: in Greek myth, woman-faced giant birds that snatched people away.
5. Chrysostom: (347-407), theologian, anchorite, preacher in Constantinople. The appellation means "golden mouth."

P

1. not from the rue Saint-Honoré: she was from an outlying district, not the fashionable center of the city.
2. Perfect Archangel: I am unable to identify this personage.

3. on her heart: the text has *on* ("sur") not *in* ("dans"), for a sexual slur.
4. tierce: In the early ecclesiastical division of the day, this was from 9 a.m. to noon. It had its own special prayers and hymns, as did the other divisions or "hours" of the day and night.
5. Paul: see Rom. 16:1. Cenchreae is a port near Corinth, Greece. The "Phoebe of the pagans" was a moon-goddess.
6. Pherba: not attested, to my knowledge; likely an error for Phoebe.

R

1. Radegonde: (about 520–587), Germanic princess who married Clotaire I, Merovingian king of the Franks.
2. Jericho: Joshua 2:1 ff.
3. the nickname "Rebecca": Maréchal is right, for the term comes from an archaic French verb, "rebecquer" (to argue, resist, talk back), connected with the biblical figure only through homophony.
4. Laïs: a Greek courtesan, lover of the fifth-century BCE Athenian nobleman and leader Alcibiades.
5. "Who wants to follow me...": see Matt. 19:29 and Mark 10:29. Maréchal's quotation is inexact.
6. disease: syphilis, which is thought to have been brought to Europe by Spanish sailors and soldiers returning from the New World in 1493.
7. Recollect: the Recollects are an order of Franciscan reformers.
8. wasn't the only one: During the French Revolution, Louis XVI's queen, Marie-Antoinette, and mistresses of current and previous kings were accused, with good reason, of attempting to influence governmental affairs to the benefit of themselves or their relatives. The royal couple were still in power when the *Légende* was published.

NOTES

S

1. interior will...: This was standard Catholic doctrine on rape; cf. Augustine, *City of God* 1.18-19, on Lucretia, who is denounced for having committed suicide after being raped.
2. Jacob and John: their mother is not named.
3. Sancha: (1285-1345), daughter to King James II of Majorca, married Robert I, King of Naples and Jerusalem.
4. believers: Jews and the offshoots of Judaism, i.e., Christianity and Islam. For Sara, see Gen. 12-13, 15-18:15. Maréchal counterposes the empirical faculty of sight to the irrational operation of faith, much under attack during the French Enlightenment and the early revolutionary era.
5. Tobias: hero of the apocryphal Book of Tobit, who is Tobias's father and first-person narrator of this second or third century BCE romance. The folktale incident of the possessed husband-killer freed from a demon survived down the centuries to reappear in early modern Yiddish.
6. Susanna: heroine of another apocryphal text. Lucretia is raped and commits suicide (cf. Livy's treatment of the legend); Susanna is falsely accused of adultery but rescued by Daniel's legal intervention.
7. Berrichons: i.e., she is their civic patron saint, as Genevieve is for Parisians.
8. Athanasius: (297-373), bishop of Alexandria, theologian and polemicist.

T

1. Not for nothing did Bruno Roy dub medieval literature "une culture de l'équivoque" (a culture of equivocal meaning) – a feature of French writing alive and well in the eighteenth century. Displayed in this short opening to Maréchal's T-saints, wordplay yields multiple meanings to which no translation can do justice. The second

sentence reads: "Table d'hôte desservie par les prêtres qui ran- çonnent raisonnablement leurs convives: il n'y a guère de repas plus léger et plus cher." Thus "table d'hôte" allows one to think of a restaurant or of the host (Christ's body); a "table" may be an altar; "service" may be a religious or a gastronomic event; "desservir" may mean to serve a parish or to clear away plates after a meal; "rançonner" may mean to redeem or to abduct for ransom; "rai- sonnable" may mean moderately priced or rational; "cher" may mean costly or cherished.

    The point, of course, is to represent the wafer as nothing but bread. The ellipses are Maréchal's, meant to imply illicit doings on the altar-table.

2. Crusoe: Maréchal uses Daniel Defoe's immensely popular novel, published in 1719, long after Teresa's death, as an example of the kind of exotic adventure story the young saint liked to read.
3. Index: a list of books prohibited to Catholics, established by the Inquisition in the sixteenth century. The Index is no longer enforced or added to, but it has not been abolished or repudiated, and is considered by many to be an important moral guide.
4. Empress: Theodora (d. 548) married Emperor Justinian I, who made her joint ruler with him.
5. dispute: During the early centuries of Christianity, the role of images (statues, paintings, mosaics, crucifixes, etc.) was debated because some thought that the veneration of images resem- bled pagan idolatry. Roman Catholicism emphasized the use of images to represent the humanity of Jesus, which was denied by some Christian sects. The anti-imagery (iconoclastic or image- breaking) movement was important in the Eastern churches, especially around Constantinople during the eighth and ninth centuries.
6. Molière, Corneille: the great French comic and tragic playwrights of the seventeenth century, respectively.

NOTES

U·V·Y·Z

1. born and died: Maréchal errs, for although the virgins are said to have died in or near Cologne, Ursula and her companions are from Brittany or, in a few versions, from Britain.
2. examples: the Latin names are numerical designations, probably indicating a girl's sibling position (e.g., fourth, fifth, eleventh, etc.)
3. Boileau: Nicolas Boileau (1636-1711), Parisian classicist and satirist.
4. "Non...": A slightly inaccurate quotation of line 108 from Virgil's Eclogue 3, meaning "It's not for me to settle such a major dispute between you." Even the original is ironic, referring to the taunting contest between two young shepherds.

BIBLIOGRAPHY

WORKS REFERRED TO IN THE INTRODUCTION AND NOTES

N.B. In the eighteenth century, books were often printed without a date, without a publisher's name or place of publication, or with a false place of publication. I have kept Roman numerals where they appear on a title page.

Aubert, Françoise. *Sylvain Maréchal: Passion et faillite d'un égalitaire.* Pisa: Goliardica; Paris: Nizet, 1975.
Baillet, Adrien. *Les vies des saints et l'histoire des festes et des mystères de l'église composées sur ce qui nous est resté de plus authentique, de plus asseuré & de mieux établi dans leur culte....* Paris: Jean de Nully, 1710.
Boswell, John. *Same-Sex Unions in Premodern Europe.* New York: Villard, 1994.
Buonarroti, Philippe. *Buonarroti's History of Babeuf's Conspiracy....* Trans. Bronterre O'Brien. London, 1836. Reprint, New York: A.M. Kelley, 1965.
Burrus, Virginia. *The Sex Lives of Saints: An Erotics of Ancient Hagiography.* Philadelphia: University of Pennsylvania Press, 2004.
Bynum, Caroline W. *Holy Feast and Holy Fast: The Religious Significance of Food to Medieval Women.* Berkeley: University of California Press, 1987.
Carlson, Marvin. *The Theatre of the French Revolution.* Ithaca, NY: Cornell University Press, 1966.
Delany, Sheila. *Impolitic Bodies: Poetry, Saints and Society in Fifteenth-Century England; The Work of Osbern Bokenham.* New York: Oxford University Press, 1998.

———. "Afterlife of a Medieval Genre: The *Nouvelle légende dorée* (1790) of Sylvain Maréchal." *Exemplaria* 22 (2010), 28-43.

———. "Bible, Jews, Revolution: The *Pour et contre la Bible* (1801) of Sylvain Maréchal," in *Festschrift for Tova Rosen*, ed. Uriah Kfir et al. Beersheva: Ben Gurion University Press, 2012.

———. "Saint Genevieve in the Revolution: Sylvain Maréchal's Counter-History." *Conserveries mémorielles* 10 (2012), n. pag.

Dommanget, Maurice. *Sur Babeuf et la conjuration des égaux*. Paris: Maspero, 1970.

———. *Sylvain Maréchal, l'égalitaire...Vie et oeuvre....* Paris: Spartacus, 1950.

Ferot, Fulgence. *Abrégé historique de la vie des saints et saintes, bienheureux et bienheureuses des trois ordres de Saint-François*. Paris: Jean-François Bastien, 1779.

Fraisse, Geneviève. *Reason's Muse: Sexual Difference and the Birth of Democracy*. Trans. Jane Marie Todd. Chicago: University of Chicago Press, 1994. First published 1989 as *Muse de la raison: La démocratie exclusive et la différence des sexes* by Editions Alinéa.

Funkenstein, Amos. *Perceptions of Jewish History*. Berkeley: University of California Press, 1993.

Furet, François. "Babeuf," in *Dictionnaire critique de la Révolution Française*, ed. F. Furet and Mona Ozouf. Paris: Flammarion, 1988.

Fusil, C.-A. *Sylvain Maréchal, ou l'homme sans dieu...*. Paris: Librairie Plon, 1936.

Hesse, Carla. *Publishing and Cultural Politics in Revolutionary Paris, 1789-1810*. Berkeley: University of California Press, 1991.

Karmin, Otto. "Essai d'une bibliographie de Sylvain Maréchal." *Revue historique de la Révolution française* 2 (1911), 262-67 and 437-43.

Kennedy, Emmet, et al. *Theatre, Opera and Audiences in Revolutionary Paris*. Westport, CT: Greenwood, 1996.

Lalande, Jérôme de. "Notice sur Sylvain Maréchal," n.p., [1803].

Latreille, A. *L'Eglise Catholique et la Révolution française*. 2 vols. Paris: Cerf, 1970.

Legrand, Robert. "Babeuf en Picardie," in *Babeuf (1760-1797) Buonarroti (1761-1837): Pour le deuxième centenaire de leur naissance*, ed. Société des études robespierristes. Nancy: G. Thomas, 1961, 22-34.

Maréchal, P. Sylvain. *L'Almanach des honnêtes gens, l'an du premier regne de la raison, pour la présente année.* n.p., [1788].
———. *Antiquités d'Herculanum, gravées par F.-A. David avec leurs explications par P. Sylvain M.* 12 vol. Paris: F.-A. David, [1800].
———. *Catéchisme du curé Meslier...l'an premier de la raison & de la liberté; de l'ère vulgaire 1789.* Paris, 1790. Reprint, Paris: Edhis, 1976.
———. "Correctif à la gloire de Bonapart," in *The Genesis of Napoleonic Propaganda, 1796-1799,* by Wayne Hanley. New York: Columbia University Press, 2008.
———. *Correctif à la Révolution.* Paris: Cercle Social, 1793, l'an II de la République. Gallica, 2007. E-book. http://catalogue.bnf.fr/ark:/12148/cb34693438b.
———. *Costumes civils actuels de tous les peoples connus....* Paris: Pavand, 1788.
———. *Culte et loix d'une société d'hommes sans Dieu. L'an Ier de la raison, VI de la République Française* [1797]. Reprint, Milan: G. Thierry, for Editions d'Histoire Sociale, 1967.
———. *Dame Nature à la barre de l'assemblée nationale.* Paris, 1791. Reprint, Paris: Edhis, 1976.
———. *Dictionnaire des Athées anciens et modernes par Sylvain M......l.* Paris, an VIII [1800].
———. *La femme abbé.* Paris: Ledoux, 1801. Project Gutenberg, 2007. http://www.gutenberg.org/files/23098/23098-h/23098-h.htm.
———. *Fragmens d'un poeme moral sur dieu.* Atheopolis [Paris]: l'an premier du regne de la Raison, 1781.
———. *Le jugement dernier des rois,* in *Le théâtre et la révolution...,* by Daniel Hamiche. Paris: Union générale d'éditions, 1973.
———. *Il ne faut pas que les femmes sachent lire, ou Projet d'une loi portant défense d'apprendre à lire aux femmes.* Paris: Gustave Sandré, 1853.
———. *Livre échappé au déluge, ou Pseaumes nouvellement découverts....* Paris: Imprimerie de Cailleau, 1784.
———. *Le Lucrèce français; fragmens....* Paris: n.p., l'an VI [1798].
———. "Le Manifeste des Egaux." N.p., [1795?]. http://libertaire.pagesperso-orange.fr/portraits/egaux.htm.
———. "L'opinion d'un homme, sur l'étrange procès intenté au *Tribun du Peuple,* et à quelques autres Écrivains Démocrates." Paris,

1796. Gallica, 2007. E-book. http://catalogue.bnf.fr/ark:/12148/cb345735668.

———. *Pour et contre la Bible*. Jerusalem [Paris]: [1801].

———. *Projet d'une loi portant défense d'apprendre à lire aux femmes*. Paris: Massé, 1801.

———. *Projet d'une loi portant défense d'apprendre à lire aux femmes*, ed. Michelle Perrot. Paris: Mille et une nuits, 2007.

———. "Une fin," in *Choix de chansons galantes d'autrefois*, ed. Paul Marion. Paris: H. Daragon, 1911. Classiques des sciences sociales, 2006. http://classiques.uqac.ca/collection_documents/marion_paul/choix_chansons_autrefois/choix_chansons.html.

Merceron, Jacques. *Dictionnaire des saints imaginaires et facétieux*. Paris: Seuil, 2002.

Perrot, Michelle. "Les paradoxes du berger Sylvain," in *Projet...*, by Sylvain Maréchal, ed. Perrot. Paris: Mille et une nuits, 2007. 93-105.

Prudhomme, L.M., ed. *Révolutions de Paris....* Paris, 1789-1794.

Robespierre, Maximilien. "Rapport sur les idées religieuses et morales: Discours prononcé à la tribune de la Convention le 7 mai 1794." World Future Fund. http://www.worldfuturefund.org/wffmaster/Reading/Communism/rob-ter-french.htm.

———. *Virtue and Terror*, ed. Jean Ducange, introd. Slavoj Žižek, trans. John Howe. London: Verso, 2007.

Roche, Daniel. *The People of Paris: An Essay in Popular Culture in the Eighteenth Century*. Trans. Aubier Montaigne. Berkeley: University of California Press, 1987. First published 1981 as *Le Peuple de Paris* by Berg.

Rodwell, Graham E. *French Drama of the Revolutionary Years*. London: Routledge, 1990.

Root-Bernstein, Michèle. *Boulevard Theater and Revolution in Eighteenth-Century Paris*. PhD diss., Princeton University, 1981. Ann Arbor, MI: UMI Research Press, 1984.

Rose, R.B. *Gracchus Babeuf, the First Revolutionary Communist*. Palo Alto, CA: Stanford University Press, 1978.

Roy, Bruno. *Une culture de l'équivoque*. Montréal: Presses de l'Université de Montréal and Paris: Champion, 2007.

Voragine, Jacques de. *La légende dorée*. Paris: Gallimard, 2004.
Vovelle, Michel. *The Revolution against the Church: From Reason to the Supreme Being*. Trans. Alan José. Columbus: Ohio State University Press, 1991. First published 1988 as *La Révolution contre l'Eglise: De la raison à l'être suprême* by Editions Complexe.
Žižek, Slavoj. "Introduction," in *Virtue and Terror*, by Maximilien Robespierre, ed. Jean Ducange, trans. John Howe. London: Verso, 2007. vii–xxxix.

OTHER WORKS INFORMING THE INTRODUCTION OR IMPORTANT TO THE SUBJECT MATTER

Andries, Lise. "Almanacs: Revolutionizing a Traditional Genre," in *Revolution in Print: The Press in France, 1775–1800*, ed. Robert Darnton and Daniel Roche. Berkeley: University of California Press, 1989, 203–22.
Brive, M.-F., ed. *Les femmes et la Révolution Française*. 3 vols. Toulouse: Presses Universitaires de Mirail, 1989–1990.
Chartier, Roger. *Lectures et lecteurs dans la France d'ancien régime*. Paris: Seuil, 1987.
D'Estrée, Paul. *Le théâtre sous la terreur...1793–1794*. Paris: Émile-Paul Frères, 1913.
Dommanget, Maurice. *Les enragés dans la Révolution Française*. Paris: Spartacus, 1981.
———, ed. *Pages choisis de Babeuf*. Paris: Armand Colin, 1935.
Godineau, Dominique. *The Women of Paris and Their French Revolution*. Trans. Katherine Streip. Berkeley: University of California Press, 1998. First published 1988 as *Citoyennes tricoteuses: Les femmes du peuple à Paris pendant la Révolution française* by Editions Alinéa.
Grand-Carteret, John. *Les almanachs français...1600–1895*. Paris, 1896. Reprint, Genève: Slatkine, 1968.
Heller, Henry. *The Bourgeois Revolution in France, 1789–1815*. New York and Oxford: Berghahn Books, 2006.

Hobsbawm, E.J. *Echoes of the Marseillaise: Two Centuries Look Back on the French Revolution.* New Brunswick, NJ: Rutgers University Press, 1990.

Jones, P.M. *The Peasantry in the French Revolution.* Cambridge: Cambridge University Press, 1988.

Lefebvre, Georges. *The Great Fear of 1789: Rural Panic in Revolutionary France.* Trans. Joan White. New York: Pantheon, 1973. First published 1932 as *La grande peur de 1789* by Société d'Edition d'Enseignement Superieur.

Livesay, James. *Making Democracy in the French Revolution.* Cambridge, MA: Harvard University Press, 2001.

Mitchell, C.-J. "La fausse intrigue: 'Londres' durant la Révolution Française," in *Livre et révolution*, ed. F. Bartier et al. Paris: Sorbonne, 1987.

Nygaard, Bertell. "The Meanings of 'Bourgeois Revolution': The French Revolution." *Science and Society* 71 (2007), 146-72.

Ozouf, Mona. *Festivals and the French Revolution.* Trans. Alan Sheridan. Cambridge, MA: Harvard University Press, 1988. First published 1976 as *La fête révolutionnaire, 1789-1799* by Editions Gallimard.

Rudé, George, ed. *Robespierre.* Englewood Cliffs, NJ: Prentice Hall, 1967.

Scott, J.A., ed., trans. and introd. *The Defense of Gracchus Babeuf before the High Court of Vendome.* Northampton: Gehenna Press, 1964.

Slavin, Morris. *The Hébertistes to the Guillotine: Anatomy of a "Conspiracy."...* Baton Rouge: Louisiana State University Press, 1994.

Soboul, Albert. *The Sans-Culottes: The Popular Movement and Revolutionary Government, 1793-1794.* Trans. Rémy Inglis Hall. Garden City: Doubleday Anchor, 1972. First published as *Les sans-culottes parisiens en l'An II: Mouvement populaire et gouvernement révolutionnaire* by Editions du Seuil.

Villiers, Baron Marc de. *Histoire des clubs de femmes et des légions d'Amazons....* Paris: Librairie Plon, 1910.

OTHER TITLES FROM
THE UNIVERSITY OF ALBERTA PRESS

The Measure of Paris
STEPHEN SCOBIE

356 pages | B&W photographs, index
Wayfarer Series
978-0-88864-533-3 | $29.95 (T) paper
Literary Nonfiction/Cultural Studies/Memoir

The Beginning of Print Culture in Athabasca Country
A Facsimile Edition & Translation of a Prayer Book in Cree Syllabics by Father Émile Grouard, OMI, Prepared and Printed at Lac La Biche in 1883 with an Introduction by Patricia Demers
PATRICIA DEMERS, NAOMI L. MCILWRAITH & DOROTHY THUNDER, TRANSLATORS. AROK WOLVENGREY, FOREWORD

488 pages | Foreword, introduction, facsimile reprint, Cree Syllabics, Roman orthography, English translation, afterword
978-0-88864-515-9 | $100.00 (T) cloth
Canadian History/Native Studies

Locating the Past / Discovering the Present
Perspectives on Religion, Culture, and Marginality
DAVID GAY & STEPHEN R. REIMER, EDITORS

224 pages | B&W photographs, bibliography, index
978-0-88864-499-2 | $39.95 (S) paper
Religious Studies/Cultural Studies